MOUNTAINS OF
HEAVEN

MOUNTAINS OF HEAVEN

Travels in the Tian Shan Mountains, 1913

Charles Howard-Bury

Edited by Marian Keaney

Hodder & Stoughton

LONDON SYDNEY AUCKLAND TORONTO

British Library Cataloguing in Publication Data

Howard-Bury, Charles, d. 1963
    Mountains of heaven: travels in the Tian Shan mountains
    1. China, Xingjieng–Uighur Autonomous Region. Description &
    travel
    I. Title   II. Keaney, Marian
    915.160441
    ISBN 0-340-52531-2   ASIA 16170

Published by Hodder and Stoughton,
a division of Hodder and Stoughton Ltd,
Mill Road, Dunton Green, Sevenoaks, Kent TN13 2YA.
Editorial Office: 47 Bedford Square, London WC1B 3DP.

Photoset by Rowland Phototypesetting Ltd,
Bury St. Edmunds, Suffolk.

Printed in Great Britain by
St Edmundsbury Press Ltd, Bury St Edmunds, Suffolk.

For
Rex B. Beaumont

Foreword

Charles Howard-Bury's journal of his travels through the Tien Shan is in a very grand tradition of imperial restlessness. The soldier-explorer was a recurring character in the heyday of the British Empire, and many of them were responsible for extending its boundaries. More often than not, though, they simply took extended leave and departed for some wilderness that had engaged their curiosity, returning months later – a little tired, noticeably fitter when they had not caught some debilitating disease, and with a fulfilled gleam in their eyes – to resume their Army careers. What's striking about so many of them is that they possessed a number of distinctly unmilitary skills, which they put to good use in their wanderings. Almost all could compose extremely readable reports. A number could sketch or paint landscapes in watercolours; and a few (like the two Robert Smiths, one a colonel, the other a captain, both serving in India) were artists of high talent. Even more numerous were the natural historians, the sub-species to which Howard-Bury belonged.

His chosen wilderness was about as remote from normal ideas of civilisation as anywhere on earth, with the exception of the two Poles. The Tien Shan range of mountains lies bang in the middle of Central Asia, which is very central and very remote indeed. These icy peaks form a natural barricade between the southern edge of the Soviet Union and the western limit of China; and, although they do not rise to the heights of the adjacent Pamirs (the so-called roof of the world), the Hindu Kush, or the Himalaya, they are a formidable obstacle at any time of the year and, in winter, quite impassable. On the Soviet side of the range, the empty flatlands of the steppe stretch away to the north and to the west for hundreds of miles before any other feature occurs. On the Chinese side of the Tien Shan, travellers have to negotiate the Taklamakan desert, which is even more intractable. There is an old Chinese legend which reckons that the Turks – who formed the backbone of Genghiz Khan's armies which ravaged half the known world – were descended from a union between a human and a she-wolf somewhere in the Tien Shan. It has never been a landscape to take lightly, in any sense. Its climate is blisteringly hot in summer and searingly cold in winter.

Coming to it from the Russian side, Howard-Bury was crossing the steppe inhabited by the Kazaks and the Kirghiz. Both have Turkic blood, mixed with other strains that have ebbed and flowed in the incessant warfare Central Asia has known from the beginning of time. Both are nomad peoples by tradition and instinct, and although seven decades of communism have changed many things in this part of the world, the tradition is far from moribund. In the summer the lower slopes of the Tien Shan, and the green valleys running into its rock and ice cliffs, can be dappled with encampments of rounded yurts, as sub-clans of the Kirghiz graze their herds of horses – bred for their meat more than anything else – before moving on to fresh pasture elsewhere. In the depths of winter on the Kazak steppe, I have seen a solitary rider on a stocky horse (he could have been one of Genghiz Khan's men, but for the rifle slung across his back) sitting watchfully over a mob of sheep, which nuzzled the snow-crust for whatever nourishment they could find underneath. Standing guard with him was a pack of extremely fierce dogs, for additional protection against wolves.

Howard-Bury went to Central Asia just after it had adjusted to the biggest change since its medieval times, and when it was on the brink of yet more upheaval. The Russians began to push south across the steppe in the eighteenth century, and by the last quarter of the nineteenth the Tsar's writ ran everywhere, bringing with it colonisation by Slavs. Four years after the Anglo-Irish soldier went a-roaming there, the great October Revolution in Petrograd and Moscow presaged an influx of Bolsheviks, who were no more acceptable to the nomadic natives than their predecessors. There was bloodshed at the advance of the Red Army, just as there had been when the Tsar's Cossacks arrived half a century earlier. To anyone who has visited the region lately, therefore, Howard-Bury's chronicle is partly fascinating because it offers glimpses of places that have since been somewhat transformed by communism. He found Semipalatinsk a grubby, dingy place, befitting its penal status; whereas nowadays it is one of the more attractively well-heeled cities in the USSR, because it is the military and scientific HQ of the Soviet nuclear testing grounds. When he reached Samarkand, where some of the minarets were leaning dangerously, he was much impressed by the colourful dress of the populace; unlike the visitor today, who finds that while the minarets have been restored to the vertical, the people have been reduced to a drab uniformity.

These, however, are not the major preoccupations of our soldier-explorer. The tradition to which he belongs is much more concerned with animals and plants than it is with politics and urban society, though he notices these things in passing, as he does even more the habits of country people, as well as the construction and decoration of their homes. Howard-Bury more precisely is one of that strange breed who can follow an animal for hours, while admiring its grace and being fascinated by its behaviour, as a preliminary to shooting it dead, very often in order to decorate a wall. Yet no-one will more surely be able to distinguish phlox from aquilegia when he finds them growing in a mountain pasture, more readily measure the dimensions of a fallen tree, more unerringly come up with a botanical or zoological name in Latin when writing up his journal.

His adventures may not have been breathtaking, but they are never less than absorbing. And there is something enormously sympathetic in our last sight of him; on his way back to Europe, together with the little brown bear he had cared for so tenderly during many weeks, and the pair of larks he had also bought in the Kuldja bazaar.

GEOFFREY MOORHOUSE

Acknowledgments

My first thanks must go to Rex Beaumont, late of Belvedere House, Mullingar at whose request I undertook the editing of the Diaries of Lieutenant-Colonel Charles Howard-Bury. The role of the late Major Walter Armytage of Halston, Moyvore, a bibliographic expert of international repute, in emphasising the importance of the documents must also be recorded. Dr. E. Charles Nelson, taxonomic botanist at the National Botanic Gardens in Dublin, was erudite and helpful as usual with regard to numerous botanical queries.

Ruth Illingworth was my able research assistant. Sean Magee reproduced the photographs from Colonel Howard-Bury's plate-glass negatives and collection of mounted exhibition prints. Olive Sharkey assisted too with the extensive volume of photographic work involved.

There are numerous people who shared with me their reminiscences of life at Belvedere during the high points of the careers of Lieutenant-Colonel Howard-Bury and Rex Beaumont, and lent me letters and photographs. These include:

Joseph McGlynn, butler to Colonel Howard-Bury and Rex Beaumont, both in Hammamet and Belvedere for a period of about twenty-eight years.

I am also grateful to Mr. Aubrey Brabazon and Mrs. Sally Young for their memories of the gardens and horses at Belvedere.

Mrs. V. M. Hutton-Bury whose late husband inherited Charleville Castle from the Colonel.

Misses Mairead and Mary Shaw, who were neighbours of the Belvedere Estate, cherish unique memories of great friendships, and were happy to share them with me.

Michael Frayne assisted in a variety of ways, giving details of the wider circle of friends of Lieutenant-Colonel Howard-Bury and Rex Beaumont.

Dublin-based journalists, Desmond Moore and the late Terry O'Sullivan, both gave events at Belvedere prominent coverage in their columns. Terry O'Sullivan compiled an extensive record of the last great charity opening in 1978 when approximately 7,000 guests came to Belvedere. Desmond Moore assisted me with further reminiscences of "Rex Beaumont of the rare blooms".

I was happy to have the assistance of Don Roberts and Joss Lynam, the father figure of Irish mountaineering.

Typing and word-processing from several manuscripts demanded the first class secretarial skills of Angela O'Brien, also Gerry O'Farrell and Frances Gallagher of Lir Secretarial Services.

The staffs of the following institutions gave me generous assistance: the Librarian and Staff, Trinity College, Dublin; the Royal Geographic Society, London; the British Embassy, Dublin; Westmeath County Library, Mullingar.

Margaret Body, my editor, gave me enormous encouragement and took a marvellous personal interest in the progress of the book.

On behalf of the Colonel and Rex, I wish to say a renewed thank you for your kind assistance.

Marian Keaney

To me at any rate, and I think to most people, whether we walk, or whether we ride or whether we drive, the most abiding joy of travel will always lie in the retrospect. The memories of some days, of some scenes where the world appears altogether too beautiful for us, where we can only gaze in awe and rapture at some marvellous creation of the Almighty, such memories as these are truly a possession which we can treasure and which will remain always to us as a source of inexhaustible pleasure and delight when we look back upon the days of our travelling.

Charles Howard-Bury, 1914

Illustrations

Contents

A Note on the Place Names

The mountains Charles Howard-Bury called the Tian Shan appear more commonly today spelt Tien Shan. But at least these variants are recognisable as one and the same range. In a part of the world where shifts of ideological power, as well as the problems of transliteration from one script to another, have produced many wildly differing names for the same place, we have followed Howard-Bury's usage as far as this is consistent. Those wanting to find Kuldja on a modern map, however, will find it disguised as Yining.

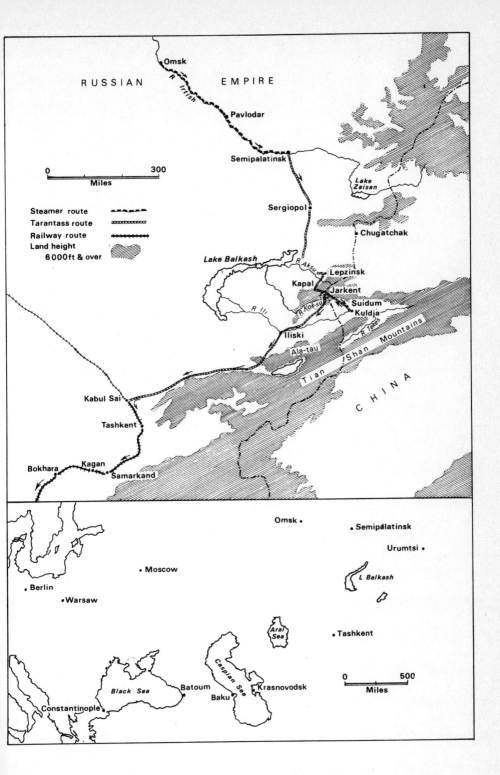

A Biographical Introduction

The diaries of Charles Howard-Bury record some unique and historically fascinating exploration in the early decades of the twentieth century. His journeys chronicle experiences on the borders of Russia under the Romanov tsars, in Ching dynasty imperial China, and India of the Raj during the waning years of civilisations which now seem almost as remote as Egypt of the Pharaohs. Soldier, intelligence officer, linguist, plant collector, photographer, big game hunter, he was blessed with lively descriptive powers, tireless curiosity, a keen eye for detail, and he has left a daily record of all his travels between 1906 and 1922, as well as a magnificent collection of photographs. After serving with distinction in the First World War, his exploratory career culminated in leading the first expedition to Mount Everest in 1921.

Charles Kenneth Howard-Bury was born in London on August 15th, 1881, descended from the illustrious Howard family, Dukes of Suffolk and Berkshire, the Bury Earls of Charleville and Tullamore, and the Campbell Dukes of Hamilton and Argyll. His father, Captain Kenneth Howard, grandson of the 16th Duke of Suffolk, had met the Irish heiress, Lady Emily Alfreda Julia Bury, on a botanical expedition in Algeria. Captain Howard of the Royal Horse Artillery had travelled extensively in India, Canada, Australia and Ireland. He was a keen botanist, gained some experience as a big game hunter, and was a competent water-colourist. On his marriage he adopted the name Howard-Bury and settled at Charleville Castle, Tullamore, the ancestral home of the Burys.

When Lady Emily Howard-Bury went to stay in London during her first confinement, her husband wrote to "My darling old wifie" almost every day, relating his accounts of attending the grand jury in Tullamore, and the shooting events in the area. He waited eagerly for the day when his wife's figure would resume its "former sylph-like proportions". When a son, Charles Kenneth, was born, he wrote to his sister, Lady Winifriede Howard, in the best fashion of Victorian fatherhood, that "the brat is enormous and ugly and it squalls like hell".

About a year later a daughter, Marjorie, was born. Captain Kenneth Howard-Bury's health was by now a matter for concern, and towards the middle of 1884 his doctors had given up hope. He wrote a final letter to his son, Charles.

> My darling boy,
> I am afraid there is no chance of my being permitted to live long enough for you even to remember me, and this I need not tell you is a very great grief to me, as I had been so looking forward to having you as my companion in my walks, and telling you all about the birds and plants, flowers and fishes like my father did when I was a little boy, and I want you to grow up a manly boy, fond of all these things as well as of your books.

After his father's death, James Keith Petty Fitzmaurice, Lord Lansdowne, was appointed guardian of Charles Howard-Bury. Lord Lansdowne, who was his cousin, was then Viceroy of India, and later to play an important role in the Foreign Office during the reign of King Edward VII.

Young Charles grew up in the splendid gothic castle at Charleville. With his sister Marjorie he was at first privately educated by a German governess and spent his holidays visiting his relatives – Lord Lansdowne at Dereen, Kenmare, Co. Kerry, his grandmother, Lady Louisa Howard, at Hazelby in Berkshire, or his flamboyant cousin, Charles Brinsley Marlay, connoisseur of Italian art, and fancier of wealthy widows, at Belvedere House, near Mullingar in Co. Westmeath. Later he was allowed further afield during holidays from Eton when his mother, Lady Emily, had a chalet in the Dolomites, and it was there that Charles learnt to love spectacular mountain scenery and hill walking.

By the time he graduated from Sandhurst with the rank of Captain in 1905 he had already travelled extensively in Europe, and now was ready to undertake his first adventure, entering the forbidden land of Tibet without consent, and earning himself a firm rebuke from Lord Curzon. However, by the following year he had equipped himself more fully for his pioneering travels. Through the good offices of Lord Lansdowne he succeeded in obtaining the necessary permits from the Russian authorities at St. Petersburg to enter the region of the Pamirs and Turkestan, while a military report, dated December 17th, 1908, outlined his suitability as an intelligence officer, and "a splendid candidate for diplomatic or intelligence work, or for any missive of secret service requiring a clever brain and active body".

The pattern of his extensive travels, on leave or on duty, was now taking shape. All the while he kept detailed diaries. He was a splendid photographer and particularly interested in the luxuriant plant life of the areas he visited. He expanded his knowledge of Indian and other oriental languages which enabled him to converse with a great cross-section of the people. His record of the religious practices and holy places of India, Tibet, Indo-China and China is fascinating. He loved to meet the lamas, high priests and guardians of these shrines and sacred waters.

In 1912, Howard-Bury inherited Belvedere House, near Mullingar in Co. Westmeath, from his cousin Charles Brinsley Marlay, and soon after decided to resign from the Army in order to devote his talents to travel and exploration. The acquisition of Belvedere House had made him a rather wealthy young man.

In the middle of 1913 he set out on the six-month tour in the remote Tian Shan mountains which is the subject of this book. His journey took him by the Trans-Siberian Railway to Omsk, by steamer through newly settled Siberia, nine days by bone-shaking horse carriage to Kuldja, and then on horseback into the mountain hunting grounds of the Kazaks and Kirghiz. It was perhaps typical of Howard-Bury's talent for ignoring difficulties that at Kuldja he added a small bear to his party. Agu (the Kazak word for bear) also travelled on a pony, not without hazard to those around him, and Howard-Bury brought both the bear and a collection of singing larks safely home to Ireland where Agu is still remembered, tethered in the arboretum at Belvedere. His master's favourite keep-fit exercise used to be a friendly wrestling match with his seven-foot friend.

He had begun preparing his diaries of this expedition for publication when the outbreak of the First World War sent him back to his regiment, the King's Royal Rifles, which he rejoined in 1915, rising to the rank of Lieutenant-Colonel. He led his men at Arras, the Somme, Passchendaele and Ypres. His diaries of this period are terse as he recounts the tragic fate of his battalion, of which there were only about fifty survivors. He himself was mentioned several times in dispatches and awarded the DSO.

After the battle of Ypres, the Colonel was taken prisoner and, although treated reasonably well by the Germans, his adventurous spirit soon compelled him to make a successful escape attempt. He was travelling north towards Kiel, moving mainly by night and eating raw turnips from ruined fields, when after eight days he fell asleep from exhaustion and woke to find a German tracker dog sniffing at his ear. He was immediately recaptured and not released until May 1919.

Shortly after the War there was a new development in the career of Charles Howard-Bury. The question of an attempt to climb Mount Everest, recognised since 1849 as the highest mountain in the world, had been deferred on a number of occasions, partly due to political difficulties in Tibet which prevented access, partly due to shortage of finance for the important scientific initiative that was planned. Now the Royal Geographical Society and the Alpine Club were taking a fresh look at the situation, and in 1920, they sent the Colonel to Tibet to superintend the complex diplomatic negotiations necessary to get the Dalai Lama's co-operation. Howard-Bury spent two months in Tibet on this mission, where his linguistic ability and the trust placed in him by the Tibetan political and ecclesiastical authorities were a major factor in obtaining permission for the expedition.

In January 1921 he was appointed its leader. The main objective was reconnaissance, though George Mallory and two others succeeded in reaching the North Col at a height of 27,000 feet, the route of all future attempts on the mountain up to the outbreak of the Second World War. Various geological, climatic and mapping surveys were carried out and among the botanical specimens brought back to Kew Gardens was a white primula named *Primula buryana* after the Colonel. The fascination of the western press with the yeti, or Abominable Snowman, also began on this expedition, when Howard-Bury asked his Sherpas about some unusual footprints in the snow.

Howard-Bury returned to England a celebrity. The one book published in his lifetime, *Mount Everest: the Reconnaissance*, appeared in 1922, and was translated into French with a glowing preface by Prince Roland Bonaparte. The Colonel was in demand to give lectures and slide shows of the expedition. But he was not a climber. He had shown the way for future mountaineers to go, in 1922 and again in 1924 when Mallory and Irvine were to lose their lives high on the mountain. But the Colonel himself had turned his interests elsewhere, entering parliament in 1923 as the Conservative member for Chelmsford.

Between 1923 and 1931 he made individualistic contributions to debates on Indian and Irish affairs, as well as the Inland Revenue, roads, forestry and local industries. He took part in the negotiations to have the Lane Collection returned to Ireland. Always a stalwart supporter of human rights, he was concerned about the persecution of Christians in Russia, particularly the Catholic Archbishop of Petrograd and other church dignitaries. However, he was strongly opposed to nationalist movements and regarded Mahatma Gandhi as a nuisance. His attempt to gain a nomination to the Irish Senate in 1925 proved unsuccessful.

On the death of his mother in 1931 he inherited further extensive property, the great castle at Charleville in County Offaly, with its acres of parklands and magnificent oak trees. The popular press noted Howard-Bury's riches and described him as a very "eligible parti".

However, while his resilient spirit and immense physical strength survived the rigours of exploration, extremes of climate, war in the trenches and life as a prisoner-of-war, a disappointment in love had a profoundly traumatic effect on him. When the lady on whom he had lavished his affections abandoned him in favour of another suitor, he regarded it as a "tragedy", the effects of which he is said never to have fully recovered from.

During the Second World War Howard-Bury met the man who was perhaps to become the son he never had. He was travelling as Assistant Commissioner of the British Red Cross and St. John Ambulance Brigade when he encountered Rex Beaumont, a young actor serving in the RAF Volunteer Reserve at Stratford-upon-Avon. Like the Arab horse in the Koran, the Lord had surely taken a breath of the south wind to create Rex Beaumont. He was flamboyant, a great raconteur and linguist, he shared the Colonel's pantheism and passion for wild and exotic places. On leave from the RAF he began coming to Belvedere which the Colonel preferred to the vastness of Charleville. Rex was soon nurturing the neglected gardens with their extensive collections of plants and shrubs brought back from the Colonel's travels. He rearranged the family paintings, and gave famous dinner parties. Howard-Bury had found a soul-mate, and their friendship was to last until the Colonel's death in 1963.

After the War the Colonel bought a citrus farm at Hammamet in Tunisia and built a magnificent villa, Dar-el-Oued, where he and Rex entertained writers, statesmen and explorers. Freya Stark recuperated there from her travels in the Sahara and Rex's donkey chewed her sun hat. André Malraux was able to compare notes with the Colonel on the temples they had both seen in Indo-China. Colonel Bourgouiba, first President of Tunisia, was a close friend.

His extravagant lifestyle, divided between Ireland and Tunisia, should not be allowed to obscure the amount of humanitarian and charitable work Howard-Bury involved himself in, for much of it was undertaken anonymously and went unrecorded. He worked tirelessly for refugees and founded a hospital for wounded soldiers on the Belvedere estate. Rex Beaumont carried on this tradition of service after the Colonel's death when he inherited Belvedere. Behind the sometimes hell-raising exterior was a deeply com-passionate man whose financial and personal assistance to hospitals and churches was vast, while he helped distressed local families to a point that eventually exceeded the bounds of prudence.

Rex Beaumont first mentioned the possibility of editing the Colonel's diaries to me in the 1970s, but recurring illness and financial problems distracted him from overseeing their progress through to publication. He died in October 1988, before the editorial work on the Colonel's diaries was completed. His death left the greatest wish of his declining years unfulfilled. I hope that the publication of *Mountains of Heaven* would have pleased Rex, and that it will help define Lieutenant-Colonel Howard-Bury's status as one of the great explorers of the twentieth century.

Marian Keaney,
Mullingar, September 1989

Editor's Note

Lieutenant-Colonel Charles Howard-Bury's Tian Shan diary fills 171 neatly handwritten pages in a canvas-backed copy-book, the cover of which bears the indelible trace of an accident with his portable ink bottle. Pressed flowers still interleave some of the pages. On his return to Ireland it is clear that he was beginning to get a book ready for publication. He had prepared the seven chapters with which this narrative opens before putting down his pen in order to fight for his country. But after the horror of the trenches it is hardly surprising the book remained unfinished.

The Colonel's enterprise and curiosity, his delight in the prospect of range upon range of snowy unnamed mountains, in alpine slopes "carpeted with Edelweiss beyond the dreams of avarice of a German tourist", his eagerness to try his luck in a gambling den, to sup koumiss in a nomad aul, or swap political scandal in a diplomatic outpost make him an attractive figure and a valuable travelling companion. It is only in his passion for hunting game that modern readers may begin to part company with him. The last two chapters of the text he prepared himself concern themselves with hunting, primarily the wild big-horned sheep of the Tian Shan, found mostly in the snows above 10,000 feet, and the Tian Shan ibex. These chapters have been edited to remove an undeniably repetitive element in the unremitting bagging of game. Though in mitigation one should remember the Colonel travelled with an entourage of up to ten men on this journey, whose diet had largely to be supplied by his gun. That said, the walls of Belvedere bear witness to this day to one of the consuming gentlemanly passions of the early years of the century.

The Colonel left some notes which suggest that, had he completed the book, it would have continued to follow the chronology of his diary and traced his homeward route via Tashkent, Bokhara, Merv, across the Caspian and the Black Seas to Istanbul and Europe. So his diary entries have been followed from September 8th to December 13th, but taking the liberty, as he did, to select the material included. The Colonel was an extremely articulate diarist and a good editor of his own material. It is only with the benefit of historical hindsight that the occasional diary entry has been interpolated into the earlier chapters.

M. K.

1

The Journey from London to Omsk

The Tian Shan mountains had for many years held a fascination for me and a consuming desire had possessed my soul to go and travel among them; their very name, the Tian Shan or Heavenly Mountains, had a suggestive sound which brought to the mind thoughts of Heaven-reaching peaks, of mighty glaciers and majestic scenery.

Unfortunately during the time that I was in India, it was impossible for me to get leave to go there. The Indian Government dislikes travellers going to out-of-the-way parts and does nothing to encourage them. They are afraid that travellers may cause trouble, if they are allowed to go and wander outside their borders and so the Government of India find the easiest and most certain way of preventing any trouble is to refuse all permission to travel in the remote districts that lie beyond their frontiers. This then was my fate when I applied for leave to go to the Tian Shan mountains, and it was not until I had left the army that I was at last able to get to that promised land, where the marvellous beauty of the scenery and the quantity and variety of game would have been a glorious reward for far greater hardships than the few that had to be undergone in order to get there.

In order to travel in Central Asia, it is necessary to be armed with a great variety of passports and permits. For the information of future travellers, I will enumerate these.

(1) Ordinary Russian Passport (obtainable through the Foreign Office in 24 hours)

(2) Chinese Passport (obtainable through the Foreign Office, but takes from three weeks to a month)

(3) Permit to travel in Turkestan (obtainable through the Foreign Office, but takes from four to six months)

(4) Permit to import firearms, ammunition and stores into and through Russia free of duty – a concession which the Russian Government kindly allows to genuine travellers and sportsmen – (obtainable through the Foreign Office, but may take from six to eight months).

The first two passports can always be obtained without any difficulty; the last two permits are the ones that cause all the trouble and delay, and which are very hard to get. Thanks however to the kindness of Lord Lansdowne and of His Excellency Count Benckendorff, the Russian Ambassador in London, I obtained these last two privately and without having to apply through the Foreign Office at all.

These papers carried me through everywhere and nowhere did I have any trouble. It is easier now for a British subject to get permission to travel in Central Asia, as owing to the Anglo-Russian Entente, the Russians have become less suspicious about us and are beginning to realise that we do not all travel for the purpose of spying and that in Russian Turkestan they have a country of great beauty, whose archaeological and historical interests are such as to attract travellers from all parts of the world.

I took as few stores as possible with me from London, as the cost of conveying them by rail and then by the post-road is very great. A valise and bedding were of course necessary, together with a camp bed, bath, etc. Through the kindness of Mr. T. P. Miller I was able to borrow his tent which he had left at Kuldja after a former journey and which saved me having to take one with me all the way from England. Baking powder and jam in tins had to be taken from London, as neither are obtainable in Russia. The jams in glass bottles that are sold in Russia would never survive the bumping in the tarantass. Photographic films, a few varieties of soups, some condensed milk and one or two delicacies such as sardines and potted meats were also brought from London. Rifles and ammunition of course also came from there.

My rifles and guns consisted of a .350 Mauser Rigby with 150 rounds of soft-nosed ammunition.

A .275 Mauser Rigby with 100 rounds of soft-nosed ammunition.

A double-barrelled 12-bore shot-gun with 300 cartridges.

The rifle ammunition was more than sufficient, as I had more than 100 rounds left over when I returned, but I much regretted that I had not taken more shot-gun cartridges, as there are great quantities of small game to be met with throughout the country.

Armed with the various passports and permits, I left London towards the end of May 1913 and, travelling via Berlin, I crossed the frontier at Alexandrovo. The Russian Embassy had informed the Custom House Authorities of the time and date of my arrival at the frontier. An official met me there who said that they had also got a telegram from the Governor General of Warsaw to authorise them to pass everything through the Customs. So all my luggage was collected, put together in one place, weighed and then passed through the Customs without anything having to be opened. A chair was brought for me to sit down upon and never have I met such polite Custom House officials. All around me were unfortunate individuals having their luggage turned inside out, and many of them were caught with some dutiable article or another, as the Russian Customs were very strict.

On arrival at Warsaw, which was only a few hours' run by train from Alexandrovo, we had to change and drive across the town to another station in order to go to Moscow. Warsaw outwardly did not impress me as a very fine city: the streets and buildings looked rather dingy and unwashed, and had evidently once seen better days.

The following evening we reached Moscow. Here I was met by John Pereira, who was to be my cook, interpreter and general factotum for the next eight months.

A slight digression will be necessary here to describe this interesting personage.

John was a Singhalese by birth and at an early age had been taken away from his native land by a Russian traveller in the Far

East. He was brought back by him to Russia, where he learnt to speak Russian, and then in the course of his service he went to Peking. Here he left his master and, joining the Russian volunteer fleet, spent the next few years as a steward on these ships going backwards and forwards on the run between Odessa and Port Arthur and Vladivostok. Getting tired of this life, he left the volunteer fleet at Odessa and, joining a travelling company of actors, he was given the native parts to act in the various plays in their repertoire. This phase of activity did not last long, and the next role in which he makes his appearance is that of butler to Sir George and Lady Macartney, the British Consul-General at Kashgar, a post which he continued to fill for some years. During this time he picked up the Turki language and the various dialects that are in use in Central Asia. On the Macartneys going home on leave, he became butler at the Russian Consulate at Kashgar and eventually accompanied the Russian Consul back to Russia. During the years that he spent at Kashgar, various English travellers had seen him and, thinking that he would prove a useful servant afterwards, kept him in mind and, on his return to Russia, Mr. Miller who was proposing to make a long trip through Mongolia and Turkestan wrote to him and asked him to come with them as interpreter and cook. On this trip he proved of the greatest help and assistance, and it was through Mr. Miller that I was able to get hold of him to accompany me. I was very lucky in being able to do so, as the number of men that know Russian, Chinese, English and the Central Asian languages is very scarce. He proved of the greatest use to me as, not only was he very hardworking and an excellent cook, but he had also a wonderful way of getting on with the natives and smoothing over difficulties.

In Moscow I bought a few more stores: excellent tea can be obtained here and so I laid in a good supply to last me all the time that I was away. There are some fine stores in the town, where almost anything can be bought, but the prices are nowhere low.

The Kremlin and the various churches with their picturesque jumble of architecture, their gilded domes and their multitudinous colours were visited and much admired. It happened to be some religious festival, and there are many such in Russia, where there seem to be more Saints' days and holidays than even in Ireland. On this particular festival all the sick, the diseased, the lame and the blind were brought to the principal church in the Kremlin in the hope of being cured. It was the most pitiful sight to watch this crowd of suffering humanity and for the most part hopeless cases; some could barely drag themselves along, the majority had crutches, many were even brought there on beds, so strong was their faith. Faith is a wonderful force and no doubt many cures are wrought by faith, otherwise such a sad pilgrimage could not continue year after year.

Diary, May 27th
I dined at the Metropole in the evening – an excellent dinner and a good band, but I cannot escape from "Rag Time". After dinner I went to a place called the "Hermitage".

During the summer months at night the Russian appears to spend his time in one or more of the out-of-door gardens that exist in every town. As a rule admittance does not cost more than a shilling and in these gardens are performances and shows of every kind: there is usually a good play, there are jugglers, clowns, cinematograph shows, dancing rooms and numerous places where the most expensive dishes and wines can be obtained. Here consort a mixed crowd of all nationalities, and many wonderfully and curiously dressed women. These gardens are full of gaiety and life throughout the night and are curious to visit to see how the Russian takes his pleasures, turning night into day. Such a place as this was the Hermitage at Moscow, where I passed a very pleasant evening. How sad though were many of the faces when in repose and not excited by champagne. To come here occasionally is amusing, but to come night after night must get terribly monotonous.

From Moscow there were two ways open to me to reach Kuldja, in the Chinese province of Ili, which was to be my starting point for the trip into the Tian Shan Mountains. I could either go by Samara and Tashkent and then drive the 800 miles along the Southern Turkestan road to Kuldja or else I could go by the Siberian Railway as far as Omsk, then travel by steamer up the broad Irtish river as far as Semipalatinsk and drive from there due south to Kuldja. In both cases there was a drive of over 700 miles, but as the drive by the northern route was somewhat the shorter of the two, I chose the latter.

The following afternoon I left Moscow by the ordinary train for Omsk. The International Express which was to leave three hours later was so crowded, that though it does the journey somewhat quicker, the slower train appeared to be preferable.

It is necessary to arrive at a Russian station long before the train is due to start: we only allowed an hour and a quarter, and very nearly missed the train in consequence, as the buying of the tickets and the weighing of the luggage took over an hour. In this large and important station, there was only one place where railway tickets and "platzkaete" (all seats on the train are numbered and no more tickets are sold than there are numbered seats on the train) could be bought. Crowds were waiting outside for their turn to buy tickets and the man inside who doled out the tickets, took longer in making them out than even an Indian babu at a wayside railway station in India. All the luggage was eventually stowed away just as the train was leaving and I had an enormous amount in the railway carriage with me. I was congratulating myself on being alone in my compartment, but somewhat prematurely, as in the middle of the night three other people came in: there were however four berths, so that we were all able to sleep.

The next morning on awaking, I found myself at Morchansk, a picturesque-looking spot, with the countryside covered with hundreds of windmills.

A small tip to the guard now produced an empty compartment and all my luggage was transferred into it: here I remained in undisturbed possession as far as Cheliabinsk. The scenery from the carriage windows was for the most part very uninteresting, an absolutely flat country as far as the eye could see on either side, partly under cultivation and partly covered with forest.

On this train there was no restaurant car: there was however a man who came along the train selling drinks of various kinds, bread and butter and cheese, but as a rule at the halts, we had to take a hurried meal in the station buffet or else buy some eatables at the wayside stations and take them into the carriage to eat. There was no lack of food anywhere: even at the smallest station there were rows of peasant women selling whole roasted chickens or ducks, loaves of bread, bottles of milk or hard-boiled eggs at the most absurdly small prices. At each station they seemed to do a roaring trade with the passengers.

Small children at every stopping place ran along the carriages with large earthenware bowls, filled with wild lilies of the valley, selling both the bowls and the flowers for a couple of pence, so that I soon had my carriage filled with them, and as they were in water, they lasted fresh for several days and were then transferred at Omsk to my cabin on the steamer.

The time in the train was chiefly spent in reading, eating and sleeping, mostly the latter. From Ufa and across the Ural mountains, the scenery became quite pretty, picturesque wooded valleys appeared on either side, affording glimpses of rushing mountain streams, and dense forests of fir and birch covered every hill, but nowhere could the scenery be called grand, as it was all on such a small scale. Even now at the end of May there were patches of snow lying on either side of the line, for the railway gradually climbed up to 2,000 feet and the air then became quite cold.

The next morning we found ourselves across the Urals and once more on the plains and soon after we reached Cheliabinsk, the Siberian frontier, where we had to change trains: by Railway time it was only four o'clock in the morning, but by local time it was already half past six. Throughout Russia and Siberia the railway timetables keep to St. Petersburg time and, as there is sometimes as much as six hours difference between the railway time and the local time, it is extremely hard to know at what hour the train arrives at any place. Luckily there is a key to most railway timetables giving the number of hours and minutes that local time differs from St. Petersburg time and thus it is possible to work out the local time of arrival or departure for any train.

At Cheliabinsk I was first put into a very crowded carriage, but a small tip to the guard immediately produced an empty compartment, which I kept for the remainder of the journey. This first day in Asia was a very hot one, the thermometer in the railway carriages rising to over 90° F. and I was glad to shed some of my warm clothes: most of the other passengers I noticed did the same. The landscape grew very monotonous, being an absolutely flat steppe as far as the eye could reach: here and there the monotony of the scene was broken by an occasional blue lake, on which were swimming a few wild fowl. Sometimes the train would frighten away a hare, which here seem to have a much darker colour than usual, but otherwise there were very few signs of animal life.

Omsk was reached at half past two in the morning by railway time, though the local time made it some three hours later. Being so far north here, there are scarcely three hours of real darkness during the night now and when we arrived, the sun had been shining for several hours.

The railway line was now left for good and we were not to see another train for over six months. The railway station lies some two miles outside the town of Omsk, and the road from the station to the town was a most appalling one and gave me a foretaste of what to expect on the Siberian roads over which I had presently to drive for so many weary miles. The roadway was, as usual, unmetalled and full of enormous holes: as there had been no rain for some time, the dust lay inches deep everywhere and the slightest movement sent up choking clouds. In spring and autumn this road to the railway station is often impassable, as the deep holes are then covered with water and slushy mud caused by the melting snow.

To the average English traveller not much is known about the roads or the means of communication in the interior of Siberia. If he crosses Siberia, he will travel by the International Express on his way either to China or Japan, and beyond noticing the scenery on either side of the railway line and remarking the curious groups of different nationalities that appear on the platforms as he hurries by in the train, he will see but little of the life of the people and will not experience any of the real discomforts that have to be undergone, the moment that the railway line is left. The Siberian line is but a single line that links up the east with the west and to reach towns that lie to the north or the south, the rail must be left and the only means of progression then are by river steamer or by post road.

The town of Omsk lies on the right bank of the Irtish river and is a place of considerable importance. It covers a large amount of ground, but is not a prepossessing place in appearance, for the streets are long and straggling and are` for the greater part un-metalled and terribly dusty. The climate too is a windy one and the air is always full of dust during the summer months. There are no really fine buildings in the city: some of the military barracks, banks and a few of the larger shops are two-storied buildings, but otherwise most of the houses consist of only one storey and are built of wood.

The hotel to which I drove was a somewhat pretentious building outside, but all the interior arrangements and sanitation were most primitive. After four nights spent in the railway train, I naturally felt very dirty and had a great longing for a good bath. Most of the hotel servants were still asleep when I arrived, but a very weary-looking and untidy individual informed me that hot water would not be procurable for some time, as the kitchen never opened before ten o'clock!

The bath too had most unfortunately been locked away in a cupboard of which the key had been lost!

On this information being received, some of the other members of the household were roused up and after the employment of a considerable amount of strong language, a bath was eventually produced and most refreshing it was after the long journey.

Later on in the morning I went to call on [Mr. Jordan] the British Consul and his wife, whom I found installed in a very comfortable little house on the outskirts of the town. They kindly asked me to dine with them that evening at five o'clock, an invitation which I was delighted to accept.

The climate of Omsk seems to be a very trying one, as the winters there are exceptionally cold: as much as 102° Fahrenheit of frost have been registered there, and in summer the heat is often excessive and the dust most objectionable, as there is a great deal of wind and the changes of temperature are very sudden. I saw some apple trees growing in a garden, but the apples, I was told, never ripen and the trees always remain dwarfed owing to the intense winter's cold. We had a good sample of this changeable climate on June 1st. A very hot morning made me think of white suits, but in the afternoon a dust storm came on, as bad as anything I have seen in India, and the air was so thick with dust that it was impossible to see across the street. This was followed by a heavy shower which laid the dust for the time being and the thermometer dropped nearly 50° lower.

2

Up the Irtish River

Omsk lies on the banks of the Irtish river. A considerable amount of trade passes through the town during the summer months, while the river is free from ice and open to navigation, which is generally from the end of April till the middle of October.

All agricultural implements and farm utensils have to be first brought here by train: these have then to be distributed by the river steamers along the settlements scattered throughout the length of the Irtish river. During the summer months steamers ply almost every day between Omsk and Semipalatinsk and many of them are fine and large steamers. From Semipalatinsk up to Zaisan lake, the river is shallower and merchandise has to be transhipped to smaller steamers and throughout the summer a regular service is kept up to Lake Zaisan.

The steamer on which we were to travel, the *Altai*, was one of the largest and fastest on the river: she could carry a large number of first-class passengers, besides second-class and innumerable steerage emigrants: there was also quite a good restaurant on board.

The first-class fares from Omsk to Semipalatinsk were between four and five pounds: this only included passage money: the food was extra and could be paid for after every meal or at the end of the journey.

The departure of the *Altai* was announced for seven o'clock that evening. On arrival at the quay a little before seven, there were no signs of the ship, but we were told that she was a little way down the river taking in wood fuel and that she would be back in a few minutes. At length after three hours of waiting she finally put in an appearance. As she had not finished taking in cargo, the whole night was spent in loading, and the noise and the shouting were so appalling that sleep was quite out of the question. Throughout the night cargo was taken on board without a pause: fresh reliefs of men taking the place of those exhausted by the toil. This continued also throughout the following day.

Amongst the cargo taken on board were two motor cars, which were driven on to the ship, and with the petrol still in their tanks were placed close to the ship's engines, so that I fully expected a fire at any moment. The day was a very windy one and the air was filled with dust which percolated through into the cabins and made everything gritty and unpleasant to the touch.

About two o'clock the *Altai* made an attempt to start, but these river steamers, which have only a shallow draught, stand very high out of the water and expose a very large surface to the wind. The wind was then blowing with the force of a gale and the very natural result was that before we could get properly started, we were blown with great violence across the creek into a barge loaded with wood, which smashed into matchwood some twenty yards of the third-class cabins. It was really rather a comical sight, as the whole of the outer side of these cabins was ripped off, exposing to view their surprised inhabitants inside, who appeared to be much upset at the accident. However, some tarpaulins were stretched over the exposed portions for the remainder of the voyage, a temporary and somewhat primitive makeshift, with which they had to be contented.

This accident showed how fragile these river steamers really are and that a very slight collision would send them to the bottom. The ship's officers, too, did not appear to be very capable seamen. We had perforce to remain here until the violence of the wind abated and then towards evening moved over to some wood flats to take in more fuel for the journey. The wood appeared to be mostly birch and poplar, and as the steamers only burn wood, their consumption of this very bulky form of fuel is enormous.

Hundreds of emigrants had come on board, clad in curious sheepskin coats and caps: they had brought all their household goods with them, and carried boxes and bundles of all shapes and sizes containing their valuables. They were a queer looking and unwashed crowd, and the smell of crowded humanity on the lower decks was not pleasant. They were all on their way to the southern parts of Siberia where the Russian Government is rapidly establishing colonies in the fertile lands adjoining the Chinese frontiers.

The emigrants mostly come from the over-populated districts of southern Russia, where famines are frequent, and to these people with their families the Russian Government gives free passes over the railways, pays half their fares on the river steamers and gives them a grant of about forty acres of land at the end of the journey. I was destined later on to see a good deal of these colonists and to travel for hundreds of miles through a country that was in the process of being colonised, and very interesting it was to watch the different stages of progress made by colonists who had been out there for two, three or four years.

The cargo on these river steamers consisted almost entirely of agricultural implements for the various colonies that are being formed in the South and the demand for these is naturally enormous. Throughout the winter months, when navigation on the river is impossible, vast stores of these rapidly accumulate at Omsk, and so, as soon as the river is free from ice, every steamer is laden to her full capacity with all the different variety of implements that a new agricultural population needs and thus during the summer no steamer is ever in want of a freight.

Eventually after a delay of over twenty-four hours, the *Altai* finally left Omsk. We had already travelled far enough to the East, for time to be a matter of little account. The journey up the Irtish river from Omsk to Semipalatinsk, a distance of over 1,000 versts (600 miles) took five days, as the current was very strong.

I awoke feeling very cold, the first morning on the steamer, as the one blanket that the Company provides to each passenger is only a small one and one's feet protrude well beyond it. Outside there were only grey skies and all day long a cold rain and sleet fell. There were many stops at small wayside stations and sometimes too we stuck on mud banks which caused considerable delay and it would only be after much shouting and pushing that the ship got off again.

The river is about half a mile wide, and the country on either side is flat and most monotonous to watch. At this time of year the river is in flood from the melting snow and has overflowed its banks for several miles, with only the tops of a few willow trees showing above the water here and there.

The Fourth of June was spent on board, but there was no other old Etonian there with whom to celebrate the occasion. My fellow passengers, though otherwise well educated, were unfortunately ignorant of all languages except Russian, though I eventually found one prospector who had a knowledge of a few words of German. The reason they gave me for learning no other language but Russian was that Russia and Siberia were such vast countries that they could travel for two weeks by train and for months by post road and need no other language, so wherefore was the use of learning either French or German.

Luckily I had a plentiful supply of literature with me and so the time passed quickly. The second day on board was again cold and wet, and there was a strong north wind blowing: there were still patches of snow on the banks, but often, as far as the eye could reach, the country was all under water, with here and there a few houses or hay ricks standing up out of the flood. The bird life however was very interesting and we passed numberless swans, duck, geese and teal, which flew away at the approach of the steamer. I noticed, too, several swans' nests perched up on the top of some of the hayricks that just protruded above the water.

Many of my fellow passengers were going on to Mongolia where Russian influence and prestige stands very high at present, and where they were going to prospect for minerals, but chiefly for gold and coal, of which it is known that there are large deposits just over the Mongolian frontier. From Semipalatinsk they travel by a different route to the one where I am going, as they are continuing their journey for several hundred miles more up the Irtish river.

The following morning we arrived at Pavlodar, a rather larger village than any we had seen since leaving Omsk and here we dropped a good many of our passengers. A large amount of cargo had to be unloaded and we stopped here for six hours. The rain had at last stopped, but the bitter north wind was still blowing strongly and, as one of the local inhabitants remarked, there are eleven cold months here and only one hot month, a fact which certainly seemed to be true. The country, which is treeless, has a bleak and windswept look about it and even in this month all the people wear curious fur caps with flaps that let down over their nose and ears and which are tied up under the chin in order to protect them against the icy winds that sweep over these plains all the year round.

Many of the villages that we passed, at present half-buried in the water, are inhabited by the Kirghiz in winter, who come here to catch fish through the ice. But at the present time the Kirghiz are scattered all over the plains, living in their yurts and grazing their flocks and herds on the rich grass that springs up everywhere on the steppes as soon as the snow has melted. In the summertime, when their ponies are well fed and in good condition, they hold great racing matches over the steppes, the distances being as much as 30 versts (18 miles) – a very different length of course to that of any of our flat races. All the neighbouring villages come over to take part in these local race meetings and there is much betting on the result and much merrymaking and drinking of koumiss as well, for by nature they are thoroughly cheery fellows and come prepared to enjoy themselves.

An exceptionally good racing pony will fetch as much as 100 roubles (£10), but quite a good pony can be bought for 50 roubles (£5). The ponies are small but very hardy, and capable of travelling great distances during the day: it is by no means an uncommon thing for a pony to be ridden 150 versts (90 miles) in the 24 hours. The ponies are generally unshod and are remarkable for the exceptionally hard quality of the bone in their hoof.

There are not many good furs to be bought in these districts: pony skins are common and so are fox and wolf skins, but other varieties of fur are rare. The Kirghiz kill most of the foxes and wolves by poison, but they have also a curious method of hunting the wolf which abounds in these districts. This method can only be employed in winter when the snow is soft. Ten or twelve Kirghiz will collect, mounted on their small wiry ponies, and on finding a wolf one man will start off and ride after the wolf driving him gradually round in a large circle: when the circle is nearly completed, another man will take his place and try and drive the unfortunate wolf round again in a circle: this game is repeated several times until the wolf is thoroughly tired out and unable to go any further, when the hunters can then ride up to him and knock him on the head with their sticks.

Oh, the dreariness of some of these wayside stations at which we stopped, a barren wind-swept plain, a few yurts and maybe a couple of wooden huts were all that was to be seen: for hours we would stop and dump cargo down on to the bank for it to be carried away later by unseen persons from distant villages. At many places there were large heaps of slabs of salt, which looked like dirty snow, that had been cut out from the salt lakes that lie close to the river, in slabs of about a foot to eighteen inches in thickness.

During these wearisome halts, when not watching the throng of different nationalities and colours that lined the bank, I would pay a visit to some of the Kirghiz yurts, which look extremely comfortable and warm inside. Built in a circular shape, they have a wooden framework inside over which is stretched white felt made from their flocks and tied down carefully with rope outside to withstand the furious gales of winter. An opening in one side has been left for a door, over which a mat is let down: in the centre of the circular roof there is a large opening, partly to give light to the interior and partly to let out the smoke. In the middle of the yurt is the fire round which sit the family or guests, while they talk or partake of refreshments. The walls around are decorated with coloured blankets and embroideries, some of which are extremely pretty: the blankets and the bedding of the family, together with some brilliantly coloured boxes containing their personal clothing, are ranged round the foot of the walls and the whole effect is very pleasing. It is wonderful how warm these yurts are inside and how they manage to survive the terrific gales. Centuries of experience must lie behind them.

The steamer plods along southward steadily, when not stopping to load or unload cargo, and the next morning we awoke to find ourselves in quite a different climate. The thermometer rose to 90° Fahrenheit and though the wind blew with great violence during the middle of the day, it was a hot and dry wind.

To laze on deck and watch the bird life formed a delightful occupation. The river still remains nearly as wide as it was at Omsk, but the navigable channel for steamers is very much narrower: it is, however, well buoyed here with red and white buoys, and here and there are signal stations which show the correct channel, as when the river is in flood and has overflowed its banks it would otherwise often be difficult to keep in the river bed at all.

There were fewer halts today, but at one stopping place, there were numbers of baskets of live fish in the river, some of which they brought to the steamer for sale. One kind of fish belonged to the carp family and varied in weight from half a pound to a pound in size, another kind and a much commoner fish was evidently a bottom feeder. It was narrow and thin and had a long kind of pointed beak underneath its head. Several inches from the end of this beak was its mouth and in front of the mouth were four little feelers or suckers: these fish varied in size from half a pound to about three pounds in weight. I bought one and had him cooked for dinner and he was quite good eating.

On June 7th we reached Semipalatinsk after five days spent in the steamer: these big steamers only go up the river as far as Semipalatinsk and then return back again to Omsk. There is, however, almost a daily service between Semipalatinsk and Zaisan, another five or six days farther up the river, but the steamers are much smaller and draw less depth of water.

The last few miles of the river before reaching Semipalatinsk were quite pretty. It was a beautiful summer's day and blue hills appeared faintly in the distance: on either bank were growing fine large poplar trees.

We passed close to one picturesque little village on the side of a hill, with its green roofs and blue domes shewing just above a fine clump of poplar trees. There are some hot mineral springs here, where people come to take the waters and before many years are over, we may find this place becoming the Carlsbad of Siberia.

The river now contracts in width considerably and the banks become much higher: the vegetation too quite changes in character:

45

flowering shrubs appear on both banks and the air is scented with perfume.

At last we arrive, after a great deal of whistle blowing, at the wharf of Semipalatinsk and our river journey is at an end.

3

Siberian Post Roads

The moment that I stepped on to the landing stage at Semipalatinsk, I was stopped by a policeman, who seeing that I was a stranger to those parts, asked me my name and business there. Giving him my card and showing him the permits to travel in Turkestan, I was allowed to go to the Hotel, while the Chief of the Police was to be consulted on the subject. Shortly afterwards a Sergeant of Police arrived, who took away our permits and passports in order to examine them at leisure. These proving to be quite satisfactory, I was then given permission to start whenever I wanted.

The Pavlovski Hotel had been recommended to me as the newest and the least filthy in the town, but on arrival there, I found all the rooms occupied: a small and empty larder next to the kitchen was eventually put at my disposal and into this I bundled all my kit: as I had a camp bed, a table and chair, I was independent of any hotel furniture and so managed to pass the night fairly comfortably.

The town of Semipalatinsk had a most unattractive appearance and to have been exiled for life there, as were many well-known Russian political prisoners, must have been a dreary penance. The town is situated for the most part on some sand hills on the right bank of the Irtish river: there are actually sand dunes in the streets, and as the place has a great reputation for wind, it naturally follows that it has also the unenviable notoriety of being the dustiest place in Siberia. The town is of good size but very straggling: the houses are nearly all built of wood and are of only one storey: the number of two-storied buildings could be counted on the fingers of one's hand. By far the finest building in the town is the Palace of the Governor of the Province, which is surrounded by trees and gardens.

The first afternoon in Semipalatinsk was spent in shopping and in trying to buy a tarantass for the long drive across the steppes. After much consideration, I had eventually come to the conclusion, that it would be advisable to buy a tarantass, so as to avoid the bother of having to change at every post station, which would otherwise have been the case. As I had a considerable amount of kit and stores the trouble of having to pack and unpack these after every few miles seemed to make the purchase of a tarantass very desirable. This purchase I never afterwards regretted: it added immensely to the comfort of the long drive to Kuldja and on the return journey to Tashkent, and I was eventually able to sell it for not much less than I had originally paid for it.*

To those unacquainted with the exquisite instrument of torture called a tarantass, a few words of description may be here necessary.

The tarantass is a conveyance on four wheels, but without springs of any kind: in order to break the rude shocks and the severe bumps caused by the holes and the inequalities of an unmetalled cart track, it has to rely entirely on the pliability of the almost rigid poles on which the body is fastened. Any conveyance fitted up with springs would be broken in a very short time, as the horses generally go at full gallop, no matter what the condition of the so-called road may be. The body of the vehicle is a basket covered with leather and having a leather hood as a protection against the weather. The bottom of the basket is filled with hay and on this is placed the traveller's rifles or other flattish boxes or luggage that he may have: on the top of this the bedding is spread out and on this the traveller reclines, only to be shot up and down or from side to side like a pea in a drum. Other boxes are tied on behind the body on the poles on which the body rests and which stand out behind for three or four feet. Three horses are harnessed abreast to each carriage, one between the shafts and two outside: the horses are as a rule in

---

* Howard-Bury's diary expands on this transaction: "John had to change tarantass at every station, as I only bought one, but most of the heavy luggage is on mine and so does not need shifting every time."

very good condition, as they are well looked after and not over-worked, and the drivers are very skilful at their job.

The tarantasses that are kept at the post stations for the traveller who has not one of his own are the most antiquated old vehicles: few of them have hoods and so every shower of rain falls directly on to the occupant. Many of the carriages that I met on the road would prove objects of interest to any museum, so ancient looking are they in appearance, and one would almost say that they had been in use since the days of Marco Polo.

In my efforts to buy a tarantass, I first went to the Post Office, where they had several miserable looking tarantasses for sale, but the prices that they asked for these antediluvian vehicles were ridiculous. I then went round to several warehouses and shops, where I was told that they had secondhand ones for sale, but the prices that they asked for these were considerably more than the article was worth when new. It seemed to be that the older a carriage was, the greater was the value set upon it by its owner. The fact that I was an Englishman and a foreigner sent up the prices everywhere.

At length I came to a coachbuilder, and on asking him if he had any tarantasses for sale, he produced quite a number of new ones; for these he was only asking 160 roubles (£16), a price which seemed quite reasonable and which was very much less than what other people were asking for their secondhand ones. It was not long therefore before we came to terms. There were one or two more fittings to be added on, such as a shoe for the back wheel on steep hills, and he promised to have the tarantass round at the Hotel the following morning.

That evening after dinner, I wandered round to the public gardens to listen to the band: the music was, however, very poor, as most of the instruments were out of tune. The gardens themselves were quite pretty and filled with a shrub that was covered with small white flowers, but which were without scent, a species of Lonicera. There were crowds of people walking about, but the mosquitoes were very active in their attentions, so that I soon beat a retreat to the Hotel where there were none. This was the last good night's rest that I was to enjoy until I reached Kuldja ten days later.

It was not till after mid-day on the following day that the new tarantass arrived round at the Hotel: immediately after its arrival I sent John round to the Postmaster to ask for horses. Being annoyed that we had not bought one of his old tarantasses, he replied that he had got no horses available. How I grew to know and to hate those words later on! The horses were at the post station all right, and only the day before he had said that he had always any number of horses available. With some difficulty however we managed to hire private horses for the first stage of 25 versts, though at a much enhanced rate.

The average expense of the drive works out at about 5 kopecks (1¼d) for each horse per verst: this includes tips to the drivers, all food on the way and any little incidental expenses that may crop up. The actual Government charge for each horse is 3 kopecks (¾d) per verst. On some of the less frequented post-roads, Russians can usually manage to get three horses and only pay for two. The driver is changed after each stage and expects a tip of from 15 to 30 kopecks (4d to 7½d) and the larger the tip the faster will he make the horses go.

We eventually managed to get away from Semipalatinsk about five o'clock that afternoon: after going for about a mile we came to the bank of the Irtish river which had to be crossed by ferry. The river at this point has an island in the centre of it, which divides it into two channels, two hundred and three hundred yards wide respectively. Each of these branches is crossed by a ferry boat swung from a number of boats anchored up stream, the current carrying the ferry boat across. The boats are very capacious and can carry half a dozen carts at a time, together with all their horses and passengers.

Once on the left bank of the Irtish, the horses started off at full gallop and all signs of the town were soon left behind and the flat steppe extended around as far as the horizon. At first there was a certain amount of grass, but this soon gave place to wormwood. The going was on the whole not bad as the plain was very smooth and by avoiding the old tracks there was not much dust.

The first stage of 25 versts was soon accomplished, and after drinking some tea and eating some boiled eggs at the post-house we were given fresh horses and that evening covered another stage, a total of 47 versts from Semipalatinsk. By this time it was half past eleven and very dark; the Postmaster too refused to give us any fresh horses till dawn, so that we had to stop there for the night. I tried to get some sleep in the tarantass, but the rifle cases underneath were too hard and my legs were too long inside the tarantass, with the result that I did not get much sleep. However, after a breakfast of bread, tea and boiled eggs we started off again at 5.15 a.m.

During the summer months there is always a long delay at each post station, as the horses are out grazing on the steppe: these then have to be caught and harnessed, with the result that the traveller is always kept waiting at least three quarters of an hour. The stages on the Siberian post-roads vary in length from fifteen to fifty versts, the average length being between twenty and thirty versts. At the end of each stage, there is a post-house where there is always one and sometimes two rooms for travellers. These rooms are always kept scrupulously clean. There are no beds provided, but there is usually a sofa for the traveller to sleep upon and when, as often happens, owing to there being an insufficient supply of horses, there are four or five travellers waiting to go on, these lie down on the table or the floor, wrapping themselves up in a blanket or a coat, and to judge by the quality or the quantity of the snores, find this no more uncomfortable than a feather bed.

At the post stations, there are always samovars of boiling water to be obtained at a cost of 10 kopecks and a good homely loaf of brown bread: there is a fixed tariff written up on the walls, but if the traveller asks the amount that he owes, he will get the invariable and annoying answer, "Whatever you like." During the summer months eggs can nearly always be obtained at every post-house and these are then boiled in the samovar. Every traveller carries his own tea and sugar with him and at every stopping place where the horses have to be changed, brews himself a glass of tea. I took some jam with me as well to vary the monotony of a diet which consists of tea, bread and boiled eggs for breakfast, luncheon and dinner. Once or twice I was lucky enough to catch the Postmaster at his mid-day meal, when we were given soup, and once, as a great delicacy, a cutlet; but these were red-letter days.

The stages on the road are let out to contractors, who are under contract with the Post Office to carry the mails and to keep a specified minimum number of horses at each station. Some contractors only take up one stage, others five or six and sometimes even more. The contractors are now allowed to charge more than the Government tariff: they, however, always keep more horses than are specified as, if they did not do so, there would be a constant block of travellers on the road, since the Government minimum number is ridiculously inadequate.

The only way to get along fast is to take horses whenever they are procurable, no matter what time of the night it may be, and to travel all night, as there is no knowing when some Government official may turn up, who has prior rights over the post horses; and then after he has been satisfied, there are probably none left over.

In the matter of horses the Post always takes precedence of everyone. After the Mails come the officers and the Government officials, but as practically every traveller in these parts is an engineer or an officer or an official, or belonging to the family of an officer or an engineer or an official, the genuine traveller comes off very badly, as he has to wait till all these are sent away first, before he can expect to be given horses. This northern road is, however, luckily not so frequented as is the southern road to Tashkent, so that we were able to get along pretty well every day.

The scenery at first keeps very monotonous: there is not a tree in sight anywhere, only broad grassy plains, the undulations on which as we go along grow more and more pronounced and which finally become well defined ridges. There are a few rather brackish lakes, but otherwise water is scarce and often at the post-houses it is very salt and the tea tastes extremely nasty in consequence.

There are a certain number of flowers to be seen; a yellow, sweet scented iris was the commonest, also a species of broom and many larkspurs.

Here and there I saw a few sandgrouse and hares, but the most common animal was a small marmot who has honeycombed the ground everywhere. This marmot is not much larger than a rat, but lighter in colour and almost white underneath. He stands up on his hind legs as we approach, has a good look at us and then pops into his hole as we come near. Larks abound, too, singing for all they are worth, as the summer here is short and many a hawk was having great fun trying to catch them.

We now managed to do three stages and were then hung up at a tiny wayside Post station for over seven hours, and it was not till past nine at night that we were given fresh horses and were enabled to cover one more stage in the dark and in pouring rain. We then had to stop, as we were told that the road in front was very bad. The night too was pitch dark and the rain came down in torrents so we waited until dawn before proceeding on our way once more. However, we had covered 101 versts during the day. As I was more tired tonight, so did the tarantass feel more comfortable for sleeping in. I was only allowed however three hours and we were off again before 4 a.m. The road now was in a shocking condition after the heavy rain in the night and the mud stuck to the wheels, which together with a good deal of uphill going caused us to take three and a half hours to cover the first stage of only 24 versts.

We were now gradually approaching the watershed between the rivers that flow into the Arctic Ocean on the one side and the rivers that flow into Lake Balkash on the other side. The rise however was very gradual, though the country became more hilly. Now, too, the grass was greener and on looking at the aneroid we find that we have climbed up to 3,000 feet above sea level. A day's march to the east from the road, so the local inhabitants informed us, would bring us to ground where there are still wild sheep. Not so many years ago, there were wild sheep among the hills on either side of the road, but the advance of civilisation and emigrants have driven them further afield.

All day long we passed strings of emigrants' carts on their way south. They had all come from Russia and were on their way to the fertile province of Semiretchinsk, where the Russian Government gives them a grant of land. From the steamer at Semipalatinsk, they have a long and weary journey of from six to eight hundred miles, through a country where water is scarce and where what little is found is mostly brackish. The rainfall is insufficient to raise crops of wheat and, with the exception of a few more favoured localities, it is only inhabited by stray nomads.

Alternate hailstorms, followed by bright sunshine and cold winds, which made the face burn and tingle, were our lot in passing through this country. Of the emigrants that we passed, some walked beside their carts, others were lying asleep or resting inside, while many of the younger generation followed along behind, laughing and joking. When these long strings of carts arrived at any village, every available supply of eggs and bread was bought up at once, as the emigrants bring but little food along with them.

That afternoon we covered three more stages and after completing 124 versts since the morning arrived at Sergiopol at 10 p.m. The Postmaster refused to give us any fresh horses, though there were plenty available, and we had therefore to spend the night here. I remained as usual curled up in the tarantass, but as the rain came down in torrents the whole time and made a great noise on the hood, I did not sleep well. The outlook at dawn was most depressing. The sky was leaden with the promise of more rain to come and the town appeared most melancholy: it was composed of dingy and dirty-looking houses and the streets were a morass.

Such was my first view of Sergiopol. Poor unfortunate officers and soldiers that have to exist in a place like this! Theirs must be a truly miserable life here.

Everything looks sad and unhappy: the shops are wretched, the houses are decaying and falling to pieces and I was only too thankful to get away from the place.

Another road runs from here to Chugatchak on the Mongolian frontier and we met a good many Chinese merchants travelling by that road. I found out afterwards that the Postmaster at Sergiopol was most dishonest towards them: he would write the correct amount that they had to pay on their ticket, but knowing that they could not read European figures used to charge them double the amount that he had written down – a mean trick which I thought only a low class babu at an Indian railway station would practise. I never imagined a European would descend so low as this.

Near Sergiopol were a few stunted willows: these were the first trees that we had met since leaving Semipalatinsk, a distance of over 275 versts. The country everywhere is extraordinarily ugly, grey windswept hills on either side with very little grass and many stones.

For some distance we followed the valley of the Aksu, crossing and recrossing the river. There were no bridges over it anywhere: the water, however, was luckily no more than eighteen inches deep, as it was not yet in flood, in spite of the heavy rain. The going was sandy and at times a great strain on the horses. Near the river were occasional small poplars and willows, and the shrub with white flowers belonging to the honeysuckle family, though without any smell.

About mid-day we came in for a terrific hail and thunderstorm: the hail came down with such violence that nothing could keep it out of the carriage and the horses turned round and refused to face the storm. This happily did not last for more than half an hour, but the ground was white for some hours afterwards. All day there were storms wandering round, but this was the only one that caught us badly. The dark and sombre cloud masses were at times very impressive, and throughout the day there was a constant rumble of thunder in the air.

Towards evening we got into flatter country again, where the plains were covered with wormwood as far as the eye could see. Up till midnight we had covered 140 versts which was quite good going. As the road now lay over a flat country, we continued travelling all night, but at eight o'clock in the morning had only succeeded in covering 32 versts since midnight, owing to the sandy nature of the soil which made anything faster than a slow walk impossible.

We had to cross several arms of the desert which stretched across the road from the west in broad rivers of sand several miles wide.

There are a good many wolves in these parts, I am told, but they do not cause much damage, as there are so few herds and flocks in this barren land. On these plains gazelle are also to be found in considerable numbers. We now had to cross a range of rocky hills, in which there are still said to be wild sheep: from the description given me, I should think they were a kind of oorial. We are now not far from the shores of Lake Balkash, an immense inland lake: in the vast reed-covered districts towards the western end of the lake tiger are to be found, but at the eastern end there are only wild pig and wolves. In the spring, when the ice begins to melt, there is extremely good fishing to be got at this end of the lake where the Sergiopol river flows into it.

The scenery is still terribly ugly and monotonous: low rocky ridges alternate with broad grey and yellow plains. Everything is of one colour: vegetation and the soil on which it grows, both are alike; there is no grass, only wormwood and a kind of dwarf gorse.

Before we reached the third post station today, and luckily when only 3 versts from it, the axle shaft of the second tarantass broke and I had to go on to the station and send another tarantass back into which everything had to be transferred and the broken tarantass was left as a wreck by the roadside.

Further on the plain became at times as white as snow from the alkali in it that had come to the surface. The going was now very bad and I was jerked up and down and from side to side all day. Towards evening we got our first glimpse of lofty snow mountains to the south. Now I welcomed their appearance, dim shadows as they were at first and hardly to be distinguished from clouds. On the far side of them were to be my happy hunting grounds, over which I was to wander for the next six months.

There was still some way to travel before we could reach the foot of the mountains and meanwhile the going was very sandy and heavy. We kept crawling slowly up and down over big sand dunes, when all of a sudden in the midst of the sand, we came across a fair sized river on the far side of which, across a wooden bridge, stood the town of Lepzinsk, set in a bower of green. What a delightful contrast!

The air was now sweet with the scent of a flowering tree, the thorny boughs of which were covered with sweetly scented yellow flowers. (*Eleagnus orientalis.*) There were pleasant grassy meadows all around, well irrigated and with many a wild flower growing on them. The contrast to the barren country through which we had been passing made Lepzinsk look doubly beautiful.

From now on to the mountains, the rainfall is greater and the climate milder, so that vegetation becomes everywhere more luxuriant. After leaving Lepzinsk we covered a couple more stages before midnight. On this day we covered 153 versts, which was the greatest distance covered in one day on the post road either going to Kuldja or on the return journey to Tashkent.

We kept on all night, though in the early hours of the morning, it needed much argument on John's part, as well as the gift of a rouble to induce the Postmaster to give us horses. He was not anxious to get up and to leave his warm bed, so he swore at first that all the horses were away, but after much grumbling they were eventually produced. It took us then ten hours to do 47 versts, as we had to cross a range of rocky hills that formed a kind of buttress to the snowy Ala-tau mountains.

The road, such as it was, followed the bottom of a narrow and stony gorge which contracted at times to but little more than the width of the tarantass and in places the gradient was most dangerously steep.

On the slopes on either side were masses of red and yellow poppies, while out of the crevices in the rocks sprang bushes of yellow or white briar roses.

On arrival at the top of the pass, which was only about 4,000 feet in height, there was a glorious view of the snowy mountains, only separated from us now by a narrow grassy valley. The outlines of the mountains were soft and rounded and unlike the amazing rocky peaks of the Tian Shan. No trees were visible on the slopes, but in the valleys and in sheltered spots were forests of fir trees. The sun was shining brightly and soon from nowhere fleecy clouds appeared and drifted in white masses along the upper slopes of the mountains. From now onwards, the road kept at the height of over 4,000 feet and we drove across beautiful grassy meadows covered with gentians and alpine flowers, and dotted over with flocks of sheep and goats or with here and there herds of horses and cows enjoying the rich sweet pasturage.

Soon after mid-day we arrived at Kapal, a prettily situated town with quite a large military garrison. The town is surrounded by trees and lies at the foot of the northern slopes of the Ala-tau. The streets are well laid out, but the houses are small and are all built of wood brought down from the forests in the mountains. It should, however, prove a pleasing station at which to be quartered.

Small game abounds in the neighbourhood; I saw numbers of

chukar (*Caccabis chukar*) by the side of the road, also a good many wild duck and partridges, whilst in the mountains close by are bear, ibex, roe-deer and wapiti, and on the far side of them are to be found *Ovis ammon karelini* and gazelle, so that to anyone fond of shooting, this would be an ideal spot at which to be quartered. The average Russian officer is unfortunately not fond of it and so finds life here very dreary at this distance from the civilisation of large towns.

Having had rather a sore throat for the last few days, I went to the local chemist about two o'clock in the afternoon to try and get some lozenges, but found the shop locked up, and on enquiry I found that it was only opened from nine till twelve every day as the place was a very healthy one and there was never much work to do!

Except for a few trees at Sergiopol and Lepzinsk, this is the first place in the 650 versts that we have traversed since leaving Semipalatinsk, where they are at all plentiful.

We were delayed here for over eight hours, as at first there were no horses available and we only eventually managed to get off late that night by bribing the Postmaster heavily, as officials and Government clerks kept arriving from both directions, who were entitled to ponies before we were. That night we only managed to do one more stage, having to stop at one in the morning, as the Postmaster refused to give us horses for the next stage until daylight. Owing to the long delay at Kapal, we only managed to do 105 versts during the day. I am beginning now to get more accustomed to the tarantass and can manage to get a certain amount of sleep during the night, only waking up at very bad bumps.

The first stage in the morning was a very pretty one, over a delightful grassy country: the sun shone brightly and warmly, and we are no longer tormented by the cold winds of the northern steppes.

Dotted over these grassy downs were numerous Kirghiz and Kazak auls. Small boys on horseback were to be seen everywhere looking after the countless camels, horses, cows, sheep and goats that were scattered about feeding on these rich pastures.

Some miles farther on we passed through numerous settlements of Russian moujiks: some were already settled and living in clean whitewashed houses and were busy now ploughing their land, others, who had only just arrived, were starting to build their houses. The walls were composed of soda, plastered over with clay outside and inside and then whitewashed: not a very permanent form of habitation in a country where there are bad earthquakes, but at the same time they can easily be built up again.

At one of the post stations, the Postmaster strongly objected to my bringing my basin indoors to wash my face and hands: such a thing, he said, had never been done before and if I wanted to wash, I must go outside!

The next stage was a hilly one and very dusty, but we covered it at a good pace, as the drivers were good though very reckless and we went at full gallop down several extremely steep hills, where there were sharp turns to be made at the bottom and we were very lucky to arrive at the next station without an accident. Here we were held up for a couple of hours owing to a Russian General passing through and in consequence there were not sufficient horses for us. How I hate the sight of a uniform at any of these rest houses! it always means a long delay for us. We eventually managed to complete 120 versts before midnight, covering the last two stages by moonlight and crossing two passes, one being over 5,000 feet. The snow mountains in the moonlight looked particularly beautiful, for we are now in the midst of them.

At Kugalinsk the Postmaster was a regular bully.

Diary, June 15th
Everyone in Russia is a Government official, from the meanest clerk to the office boy, and all of them take precedence over the ordinary traveller. Here at Kugalinsk, there is a Postmaster who, because I am an Englishman, seems to take a special delight in keeping me waiting and he has not been the only one. I have already been kept in this miserable hole for over seven hours, because the wife of some clerk on a salary of 30r a month is coming.

The next stage beyond Kugalinsk was however a very pretty one, up a broad valley from eight to ten miles wide and with snowy mountains on both sides. The valley was everywhere of the richest pasture land and covered with wild flowers. There was a pretty

Campanula growing there in great abundance which was of a kind quite new to me.

We were keeping all this time at an altitude of between four and five thousand feet and were constantly passing colonies of Russian settlers which the Russian Government had planted there. Very prosperous these settlers all seemed in their neat whitewashed houses that they had built themselves and never anywhere have I seen a more healthy lot of children.

The Russian in these parts has a great look of independence about him and, on going into their houses, a most hospitable reception is always given. These valleys used formerly to be inhabited by the nomad Kirghiz and Kazaks, but the Russian settlers have now been given grants of land here, as the nomads refused to tie themselves down and settle in any one place. They prefer their independence and as they cannot get on with the Russian settlers, many thousands are every year emigrating into China.

These new peasant settlements, scattered throughout the length and breadth of Semiretchinsk will one day provide a very fine body of sturdy soldiers to guard the Russo-Chinese frontier.

We just managed to get off from the next post station in time to avoid having our horses taken for an official arriving from the opposite direction.

The road now led through grassy meadows up to a pass nearly 6,000 feet in height from the top of which we had a magnificent view over the Ili valley. This broad valley, hot and dusty looking, lay at our feet and far beyond on the horizon towered up the giant peaks of the Tian Shan. The air here is of a marvellous clearness, just as it is in Tibet, and allowed us the first glimpse of the promised land, though there were yet many weary miles to be traversed first.

We had a very steep descent now of over two thousand feet: there was no attempt whatever made to grade the road and it eventually emerged into a broad plain where there were many hares. There was no difficulty about getting horses at the next two stations and the road kept on across the plain. By this time the climate had become very much warmer, as we were now at a considerably lower elevation.

The evening lights in this brilliantly clear atmosphere were extremely beautiful, and the sunset on the distant snows was very fine. Just as it was getting dark we entered a narrow gorge, where the road rapidly descended, following for the most part the bed of the stream, where the surface was alternately loose boulders or deep sand, which made it very hard work for the poor ponies. At last we arrived at the post station, where as there were no more horses available, we had to spend the night. We had, however, during the day covered 124 versts, a very fair day's journey.

Leaving the following morning before six o'clock, the 40½ versts to Jarkent were covered in 4½ hours. The early morning was very beautiful and the distant snowy ranges stood out wonderfully clear, though they must have been more than 100 miles away. On the way many gazelle were passed, not very far from the road but sufficiently far to be out of rifle shot.

On arrival at Jarkent, fresh ponies were ordered, which the Postmaster professed to be quite ready to give us, but just as we were on the point of leaving, he informed us that we could not start until the Police had seen our passports and at the same time a gendarme came up and took them from us.

While waiting for the passports to be examined, I wandered about the town. Jarkent appeared to be a fair sized town with a garrison of about 5,000 soldiers. The town was well laid out with fine avenues of poplars along all the streets. Each house stood in its own garden and in consequence the place looked not unlike an Indian cantonment. There was one great difference however, none of the streets were metalled.

While wandering about, in one of the gardens I saw several cherry trees covered with ripe fruit. I sent John inside to find out whether we could not buy some of the fruit, as I had a great hankering after fresh fruit. The owner of the garden turned out to be a Sart merchant who said that he was quite ready to sell us some fruit and invited us inside the garden. This was a very pleasing spot on a hot day, big shady trees with bowers of sweet smelling roses; running water gurgling everywhere and under the cherry trees were luscious beds of ripe strawberries. After spending a while here we came back to the rest house laden with baskets of strawberries and cherries.

The soil here is of a wonderful fertility and, as soon as water is brought to it, it will produce anything. In the gardens of Jarkent were grown grapes, apples, pears, currants, plums, strawberries and cherries, but the fruit par excellence of this country are the water melons and the sweet melons on which the natives live for six months in the year.

On returning to the rest house to enquire whether the Police had finished with our passports, the Postmaster, who was rather a tiresome fellow and evidently wished to make some money out of us, informed us that our passports were not in order and that we should have to remain here several days.

Having no intention of doing this we hurried off to the Police station to find the Chief of Police. He was not there, but a gendarme volunteered to take us to his house and, seizing a passing cart loaded with carpets, he told us to jump on to it and ordered the driver to drive us to the Chief of Police's house, which was only a short distance away. He was having his afternoon siesta, I think, when we arrived, but after a few minutes he came out and apologised for the trouble that he had given us, saying that it was all a mistake. He then gave us back our passports and sent a gendarme with us to the rest house to tell the Postmaster to give us horses and send us on to the Chinese frontier.

There were now only a couple more short stages to be covered before reaching Khorgos, the present Chinese frontier. Here we spent the night in a small Russian village on the right bank of the Khorgos river, which here forms the boundary between Russia and China. In the evening I went round to see the Russian Customs Officer, as we were anxious to start early the following morning. He proved to be most obliging and said that he would only need to count the number of our boxes to see whether the number tallied with the number we brought in at Alexandrovo. He told us we could leave at any time we liked, and carefully examined our permits which he wanted to keep and it was only with a great deal of trouble that we got them out of him again for the return journey. Poor man, he has been here for two and twenty years, working day and night and with never a holiday all this time.

We roused him up at four o'clock in the morning when we started, but he did not seem to mind it.

Immediately after leaving the Custom House, the road descended a steep bank into the bed of the Khorgos river, which was very stony and nearly a mile wide. The river which was extremely muddy from the melting snow was at its lowest at that hour and was luckily divided up into a number of small streams: we had to ford all these as there was no bridge and even now some of them were pretty deep.

We now entered Chinese territory, passing under a large crenellated gateway built of dried mud. The whole atmosphere now seemed to have changed and we could not help feeling that we were at last in the real East.

Under the gateway were reclining a few Chinese soldiers who lazily asked for our passports. A sleepy official then proceeded to examine them and spent some twenty minutes in copying them into his book after which permission was given us to proceed.

After going a few versts, we came to a town surrounded by a mud wall. Here we stopped in the main street outside a Chinese tea shop and had some tea and bread, much to the interest of the local inhabitants, who soon formed a curious crowd round the tarantass. The Chinese bread is not at all unpleasant to the taste: it is made in the shape of a chupatti, but larger and thicker and much lighter.

After breakfast the road, such as it was, led through a very fertile and well irrigated part of the country, passing however on the way numbers of ruined villages, showing that the population here at one time was very much greater than it is now.

After covering 50 versts, we arrived at Suidum, a fairly large Chinese town surrounded by mud walls and here horses were changed. There was a Cossack detachment in the town and the officer in command kindly invited me to come in and take a cup of tea with him, which I was very glad to do. He was living in rather a tumbledown house but he had nice carpets round the walls. He could only speak a few words of English and as my knowledge of Russian was very limited, our conversation was only carried on with much difficulty.

It was now only another 44½ versts on to Kuldja, the end of the so-called driving road, and this lay across a very hot and dusty plain. This last stage we covered during the course of the afternoon.

How I did welcome the end of the journey in the tarantass! During nine days, we had driven nearly eleven hundred versts, being bumped and shaken all the time and only snatching an uncomfortable sleep in the intervals. It was, however, an experience never to be forgotten.

4

Kuldja

The town of Kuldja [modern Yining] is in the old province of Ili, one of the remotest provinces of the Chinese Empire. It used to be well-known to diplomatists for various reasons in the days before telegraphs were brought there. The Chinese Government whenever it wished to delay matters or when it was not particularly anxious to answer some tiresome diplomatic question, used to refer the matter under dispute to the Governor of Ili for his opinion. This always meant that negotiations were delayed for several months, by which time something unexpected might have happened to cause further procrastinations. Now such methods are no longer possible as there is a telegraph line to Urumtsi and Peking on the one side and to Tashkent on the other.

The history of this province, which forms the Southern portion of the great country of Dzungaria, has been a very chequered one since the earliest of times: its geographical position has caused it to lie in the pathway of many great invasions which have swept over it, destroying the old inhabitants, but leaving fresh colonists behind. The soil is remarkably fertile and colonists have always prospered exceedingly, so that it was never long before the population became numerous again, until they in turn were wiped off the face of the earth by a new horde. If ever the history of this unhappy province were to be written, it would show a succession of wars and massacres probably unparalleled in the history of any other country. The Huns and the Mongols were each in turn masters of this country. Genghiz Khan and his hordes used to inhabit these districts, but as they were a nomadic people, they have left no buildings behind as a record of their existence here.

There are, however, relics of a colony of Nestorian Christians which existed here some 700 years ago.

About a century and a half before the present day, the Chinese invaded this country and put over 600,000 of its inhabitants to the sword, sparing neither man, woman nor child. The Chinese then found it necessary to repopulate the country, so they brought from Western China the most progressive and the cleverest of their inhabitants, the Tungans or Chinese Mohammedans. Emigrants also flocked to the land from other parts of China, as the country was well-watered and very fertile and the climate a pleasant one, and thus not more than a century after the population had been wiped out, found the country again in a prosperous condition with a large and increasing number of inhabitants.

Unfortunately, however, peace was not destined to last long in the land, for the Tungans, partly through religious fanaticism and partly through jealousy at the prosperity of the Chinese settlers, rose against the Chinese and massacred them by hundreds of thousands. The Chinese Government then sent armies which in turn slaughtered the Tungans. This orgy of massacre and fighting caused such a serious stoppage of trade with the Russian province of Turkestan, that the Russians now intervened and took over the province which they looked after and managed for ten years.

Thanks however to the diplomacy of that clever Chinaman, the Marquis Tseng, the Russians after an occupation of ten years handed back this province to China, with the exception of a rich slice which they kept for themselves as compensation for their trouble.

Though Russia had occupied the country for ten years she left few marks of her occupation behind her: she built no roads and no bridges, and the only thing that some of the nomad inhabitants learnt from her was to make hay, a thing they had never done before.

Since that time the Chinese have never returned in great numbers to repopulate the country: there has always been the fear of a fresh Russian occupation hanging over them and they did not wish to become Russian subjects. A few Chinese have however returned in spite of these drawbacks and a good many Tungans. Numerous

Sarts from Chinese Turkestan have also settled in the valley of the Ili and many of the deserted villages and cities are being again repeopled. Yet it is a melancholy sight to travel through the country and to see everywhere these ruined cities and villages that once thickly covered the countryside, with the thin bare walls of the houses marking the awful thoroughness with which the conquerors destroyed and ravaged the countryside. Time, however, is once more restoring to the country her former prosperity: the old irrigation canals are being dug out and the life-giving water is flowing once again through its ancient channels.

Wages are very high throughout the province and many Chinese come and work here for a few years, earning enough money to retire to their homes for the remainder of their life on a comfortable competence.

Kuldja and Urumtsi have always been the largest and most important towns and there has been a perpetual feud between them for the supremacy, but after the last Tungan rebellion Kuldja was so completely laid waste that she receives orders now from Urumtsi.

Russian influence in Kuldja is still all-powerful. The finest house in the town with extensive gardens surrounding it, belongs to the Russian Consul: outside the grounds in barracks live the Consular guard and escort consisting of 300 Cossacks. At Suidum, half way between Kuldja and the Russian frontier, there is also a Cossack detachment.

Throughout my stay in Kuldja the Russian Consul, M. Brodianski and his wife, went out of their way to be particularly hospitable. His work here is almost altogether political and his chief duty seems to be to uphold Russian prestige throughout the province, and during the time of the Revolution* to keep the peace as far as possible.

* This revolution was the Chinese Revolution of 1911, instigated by the northern military commander, Yuan Shih-kai, who seized power from the Manchu dynasty during the regency of Prince Ch'un, and appointed himself President of a shortlived Chinese Republic in 1912. The unsettled state of the country in 1913 is reflected in Howard-Bury's diary entry for June 18th: "There is practically no Government now in this province; everyone does as he likes, obeying no one. Opium is grown everywhere and in large quantities: robbery is rife and unpunished, for each man is afraid of his neighbour and no one dares to inflict punishment on a murderer. The Revolution has taken place here, but it has left behind it anarchy.'

There are a good many Russian shops in the town of Kuldja and a Russian church, a school and a hospital are also being built. There is a branch of the Russo-Asiatic Bank here which at present, owing to the depreciation of the local currency, is issuing its own notes for local circulation. Besides these there is a Russian Post Office, as well as a Chinese Post and Telegraph Office. The Russian Post Office, however, uses Russian postage stamps, without any writing or inscription on them to show that they are issued in a foreign country, and also, what is most annoying, charges Russian customs duty on parcels coming into China that are brought there by the Russian posts, and this duty has to be paid before the parcel is handed over.

The fertility of the province of Ili is most remarkable. The soil is a loess, which as soon as water is brought to it, will grow excellent crops of wheat, maize, millet or whatever crops may be wanted. So fertile is Ili, and so unlimited is the area of the finest soil, that in spite of its kaleidoscopic history of invasions and massacres, colonists flock back to it, like the dwellers on the slope of some volcano whose villages and crops are periodically destroyed by eruptions.

At the season of the year when the growing crops most need water, the melting snows in the higher mountains pour down torrents in such abundance that after every possible want has been supplied by irrigation, a vast amount runs wasted into the rivers.

Melons are a very favourite crop, both the water melon and the sweet melon, and in summer and autumn, the inhabitants almost live on melons. I used sometimes to gaze with astonishment at the amount a man could consume in one sitting. It is no wonder that almost every shop sells melons.

Apples, grapes, pears and apricots are also grown in great quantities, while wheat, rice, maize and various millets seem to be the staple crops. Opium too, since the Revolution, is being grown in large quantities and a considerable amount that is grown in Russian territory near Prejvalsk is also smuggled into the country. That the Russians will prohibit opium growing in their own territory is, I think, probable, not from philanthropic motives towards the Chinese, but because they are afraid that their own subjects may grow to become too fond of the drug.

The internal conditions of the province since the Chinese Revolution merit a brief review.

On February 13th, 1912, the Emperor of China abdicated and on the 15th, Yuan Shih-kai was elected at Nanking provisional President of the Republic of China. During the first year of the Republic nothing was done "to elevate the people, secure them peace and legislate for their prosperity" as had been promised them in the Republican Manifesto. The chaotic conditions which reigned in every branch of the provincial Governments and which had been gradually increasing during the last two or three years of the Empire, became steadily worse and almost complete anarchy reigned everywhere.

The old provincial administration, bad as it undoubtedly was in many cases, had some experience, some kind of authority and had been generally able to maintain a semblance of order and to collect a considerable part of the revenue of the State. The men of the Revolution of 1912 displaced the old regime and the ancient administration, and filled every office with new men, regardless of their fitness and often for a monetary consideration. Bands of brigands too preyed upon the people, terrorised the countryside and paralysed all trade.

Encouraged by promises of autonomy, the provinces kept for their own use such revenue as they were able to collect and the people willing to pay, and, notwithstanding the pressing appeals of the central Government, contributed nothing to its support.

Such were the conditions of life in Ili after the Government representatives had been removed.

At this time two men came to the fore, one Fungtaming, a small tailor by trade but an exceptionally clever and ambitious man, and the other Li Chang, who was really a dupe of Fungtaming's. These set up as Chang Chun or Military Governor, a poor, weak, old Chinaman, who had no authority whatever, and who was but a figurehead to carry out the wishes of Fungtaming. The Chang Tai or second governor of the province had strongly disapproved of the Revolution: he, however, had asked all the revolutionary leaders to a big dinner that was to be given in his house. Under the centre of the table and connected with his seat was buried a large cask of gunpowder, which he intended to explode during the course of dinner, blowing up himself and all his guests. But unfortunately one of his servants gave the secret away, and he waited and waited, but no one came to the feast that he had prepared. So during the night, being determined that the revolutionaries should never get possession of the armoury and arsenal, of which he was in charge, he went to the big powder magazine and blew it up, destroying not only himself and the arsenal, but the greater part of the town as well.

Fungtaming and Li Chang for two years then had matters very much their own way. There was practically no authority whatever in the province: everyone went about armed; murders were frequent and went unpunished; robbery was rife. Yet the guilty parties were never caught, as the rulers and the heads of the police all belonged to the secret society of the Kolahui or society of thieves, a society which is ordinarily forbidden in China, but at one time robberies became so frequent in Kuldja, that everyone was joining the Kolahui in order that their houses should not be robbed. Every man did as he pleased, he grew or smoked as much opium as he wanted; gambling houses were opened in all quarters of the city and in fact whatever the Chinese had forbidden before was now done openly and without fear of punishment.

Owing to the numerous thefts constantly taking place, armed watchmen were at night stationed in every street and there were prominent notices put up everywhere that "Good people must not go out at night": from this it might be inferred that only thieves and robbers were allowed to go out! Returning from the Consulate after dinner, I had to walk through the streets past these watchmen, but instead of finding myself challenged, as is usual in Europe, I used to hear one watchman shouting to the next to say that a stranger was coming in his direction and to be on the look-out for him and to watch where he goes. Which of the two systems is best, the European or the Eastern? I leave others to judge.

During the troublous times what little silver and copper there was in currency was concealed and buried. In spite of this, with no reserve whatever in the Government treasuries, Fungtaming proceeded to manufacture and issue an unlimited amount of notes of different values. These were printed on a cheap, common paper, but people were forced to take them: in this way several million seers of this money were issued.

Fungtaming himself used to change all his money into Russian notes and bank it in Russian banks at once. The value of the Chinese paper money became of course more and more depreciated as more and more paper money was issued.

Before the Revolution the seer and the rouble used to have the same value: in June 1913 the rouble became worth 2½ Chinese seers and by October it was worth 4 seers. The result was that anyone that had Chinese money at the time of the Revolution and wished to change it into Russian money a little over a year afterwards found himself getting only a quarter of its original value.

The price of food and ordinary articles of commerce also trebled during the course of the summer.

Besides the notes that were being issued, oblong pieces of wood or bone were used as tokens to represent money and were accepted as money in the shops. They were originally gambler's counters, but owing to the lack of currency in the country were taken into use in lieu of money.

Passing by a gambling house one day in Kuldja, I stopped and went in. There was a long table with a line down the centre and a man stood at the end with a pair of dice. Apparently one side of the table counted as an odd number and the other side as an even number. Bundles of notes were lying on either side of the line, so choosing one side, I put a rouble down to see what would happen. To my surprise I found that I had won, and besides the rouble, I was handed back several bundles of notes and pieces of bone, the whole representing apparently a considerable fortune. However, on counting out the notes and the tokens afterwards, the total amount was only about a rouble in Russian money, so much had the Chinese notes depreciated in value.

During the time that Fungtaming and Li Chang were the rulers of the province they must have accumulated a very considerable fortune, partly from bribes, but especially from this issue of paper money.

The province of Ili is especially rich in minerals, and within twelve miles of Kuldja there are five coal mines worked in a most primitive fashion by the Chinese: there is a considerable amount of copper and lead in the mountains and in places there are gold workings. A great part of the country is still unexplored and would probably afford a rich harvest to the prospector. The whole of the exploitation of the minerals in the province was to have been handed over to the Russians in return for a loan of two million roubles at six per cent. Death unfortunately stepped in before Fungtaming could sign the transaction and hand over the concession of the minerals to Russia and his successor was unwilling to agree to the terms.

While Yuan Shih-kai was only provisional president of the Chinese Republic, he had three times summoned these two self-appointed rulers to come to him to Peking and three times had they refused to obey his orders. However, the arm of the Chinese Government is long, though its methods may be slow, and it is dangerous to disobey three times.

Madoling, a Chinese general from Urumtsi, had meanwhile arrived in Kuldja and by degrees he had collected some 1,400 soldiers there, but as everything was quiet no one paid much attention to him.

On October 6th,* 1913 Yuan Shih-kai sent a telegram to the Chang Chun or Governor-General to say that Fungtaming and Li Chang were to be put out of the way. The Chang Chun, who had been appointed to that position by Fungtaming, either through fear of him or from kindness of heart, refused to do this, and sent for Fungtaming and Li Chang, showed them the orders that he had received from Peking and advised them to take refuge across the Russian frontier. This they refused to do, asserting that there was no one in the province that dared to touch them.

News of the contents of this telegram had meanwhile leaked out and come in some way to the ears of Madoling. The next morning at daybreak with his soldiers, he surrounded the houses of Fungtaming

---

* At the end of his hunting trip Howard-Bury returned to Kuldja on October 12th, at a time when much of the civil turmoil summarised in this chapter was daily news.

and Li Chang, cut off their heads and exposed them to the populace outside. The soldiers then proceeded to visit the houses of the lesser mandarins, but no one was put to death without being first made to speak. All those that spoke with the Northern dialect were spared, while all those that used the idioms of South China were put to the sword.

Madoling and the soldiers who had carried out these orders that came from Peking, were all Tungans or Chinese Mohammedans from the North of China, so that once more the Tungans have become rulers of the province.

One of the first edicts of the new rulers was to prohibit the sale of pork anywhere in the markets.

The rest of the Chinese inhabitants were very frightened at the course of events, as they remembered the Tungan rebellion of the 'sixties when everyone that was not a Mohammedan was put to the sword.

Curious to relate, the moment that the death of Fungtaming and Li Chang was known, the price of the Chinese paper money rose: the people had no knowledge that the orders came from Peking, but they thought that a new regime might be more likely to guarantee the notes. Many of the Russian traders and Russian subjects have been very hard hit by the depreciation of the Chinese money and the enormous rise in the cost of everything, so that unless the Chinese Government does something towards guaranteeing this money, the Russians will have a good pretext for interfering. Money is not plentiful at present in China, but if the Chinese do not want foreign interference in that quarter, it would be good policy for them to guarantee even half the face value of the paper money.

Such was the condition of the province during the summer of 1913.

5

Kuldja and the Journey to the Hunting Grounds

A week's rest at Kuldja was very pleasant after the terrible shaking on the post-road. A camp bed and a quiet night seemed paradise.

A few miles before arriving at Kuldja, the British Aksakal had ridden out to meet me. (The name Aksakal literally means a "white beard" and usually denotes a political agent. Here the Aksakal was a kind of unaccredited British agent to look after British trade interests.) I had telegraphed to him from Kapal to make arrangements for putting me up somewhere and he had arranged with a Sart merchant from Tashkent, who had a house in Kuldja, to lend me his house and thus I found myself installed in a very comfortable bungalow. Soon afterwards the owner of the house paid me a visit and insisted on my being his guest for that night. The house was soon filled with dalis of flowers, fruit and sweetmeats after the Indian fashion and for dinner an enormous dish of "pilau" was sent over, enough for ten men but very excellent.

A good bath that night was most enjoyable: the first that I had been able to get since leaving the steamer.

After a really good night's rest, I went to call on Father Raemdonck, a Belgian missionary in Kuldja, who had most kindly sent a man off into the mountains to try and get hold of a shikari. He gave John and myself a warm welcome. John was an old friend of his, as he had stopped with him many times before on his travels. The good Father then produced wines and liqueurs that he had made himself out of his vineyards, and of which he insisted on our partaking: they were really quite good. He then showed us round his house, his gardens, his poultry yard and finally his church, of which he was very proud, for he had built it all himself. He kept no servants, but did all the work himself. His days were very busy, for besides teaching the Chinese children, he doctored any sick who came to him at any time and if there is any one on earth that really obeys and carries out the precepts of the Christian religion, it is this good Father.

While we were there a couple of Cossack officers dropped in to have a chat with Father Raemdonck. Afterwards one of them tried to sell me a Cossack saddle, but as he was asking too much for it, we did not come to terms.

In the afternoon I went to call on M. Brodianski, the Russian Consul, who is at present the most powerful man in Kuldja and who, besides his ordinary Consul's work, has a great deal of political work to do. He had a Cossack guard of 300 men here, as well as detachments at other places. He spoke English fluently and was most friendly. Madame Brodianski, too, was a very good French scholar, so we got on well together. At tea-time she produced some excellent strawberries from her garden which covered many acres. The Consulate itself was so surrounded by tall trees, which at this time of year gave a most grateful shade, that it was hard to imagine we were in a large town, so rural were the surroundings. After tea tennis was played on a mud court in the garden. M. Brodianski had only just introduced the game into Kuldja, so that none of the officers or players were very proficient, nor was the court smooth: it appeared to have been ridden over, as it was full of holes but, in spite of this, they all appeared to enjoy the game.

The following day was spent in the Kuldja bazaars, bargaining and shopping. All the many requirements for camp life had to be collected that would have been too bulky to have brought with us on the tarantass over the post-roads from Europe.

We were able to borrow some of Mr. Miller's tents that had been left in Father Raemdonck's care and which he had most kindly given us permission to use.

The flies in Kuldja at this time of year were very tiresome, but we managed to rig up some kind of fly papers in the bungalow which did great execution among them. The sun now in the middle of the day was very hot, but inside the houses the temperature was nice and cool, and the nights were very pleasant.

In the evening, Father Raemdonck and I went to supper with M. and Mme. Brodianski. We had a very cheery meal out of doors under the trees and it was past midnight before we left the hospitable Russian Consul and his wife. Cossack guards opened the garden gates for us and let us out.

The next few days were spent in shopping and in interviewing horse dealers. Very few of the latter had yet arrived at Kuldja and those that were there, were asking too big a price.

There is an old and a new town at Kuldja, but few interesting buildings in either of them. The old town is surrounded with high crenellated walls and imposing gateways, but beyond a few yamens [official buildings], the buildings there were of a squalid and deserted appearance. It was in the New Town and in the bazaars outside that all the trade was done. Here was rather an interesting Tungan mosque, looking very picturesque with its courtyard full of large trees, under the shade of which a number of small children were being taught to read and write.

On June 22nd after a great deal of bargaining with various horse dealers, one at last agreed to hire ponies at 15 roubles a month for as long as I wanted them. This was quite a reasonable price and he promised to have them ready to start for the mountains two days later. Two men, Rahmah Khan and Ashim, were to come with the ponies and look after them. I could not have wished for better men. They proved most excellent workers, absolutely steady and honest and never gave me the slightest trouble, so that it was with real regret that we parted at the end of the trip.

There was no sign, however, of Tola Bai the shikari, who had evidently not got my message, so we must try and find him at his home in the mountains.

A Russian merchant offered to give me a proper Russian bath at his house before we left, so I accepted his offer. The bath was very like an ordinary Turkish bath and most refreshing after the hot dusty days.

We had shortly afterwards a good dust storm, accompanied by some rain and thunder, which cleared the air nicely. That evening

I went again and had supper with the Russian Consul. Madame Brodianski was not feeling well, so we were quite alone. He proved most interesting in conversation and again it was not till past midnight that I left. He had spent a great many years in China and knew much about the ways and the customs of the Chinese.

Amongst other subjects of conversation that arose, I was much amused at hearing the suggestion seriously discussed that Lord Curzon was one of the causes of the Boxer Rising. Some of his speeches they said had been translated into Chinese and these had frightened the Chinese so much that they had come to believe in a White Peril and hence rose in revolt in order to drive the white man out of their country.

The ponies turned up all right on the 24th and we managed to get everything loaded by 9.30 a.m. There were ten ponies in all, including two riding ponies for John and myself.

Just before I left Kuldja, I bought a tiny bear about three weeks old, that had just been caught by some hunters and the little bear accompanied us during the whole trip and when on the march rode on the back of a pack pony, tied up between two loads.

Diary, June 24th
The first thing he did was to give me a bad bite and he turns out to be a regular little savage. He ran off too with my lunch, which I had put down for one second and he was a perfect little demon when I tried to take it back. He every now and then gives the pony a bite on the back which makes things lively.

We made quite an imposing spectacle riding down the streets of Kuldja and there was much amusement over the bear. We soon left the streets and houses behind and began passing through opium fields which were a very pretty sight as they were now in their full glory and a blaze of colour.

The track lay along the right bank of the Ili river and was not an interesting one, as there were no trees and the sun was very hot. The soil all the way was a loess and only needed water, of which there was an abundance in a thousand mountain streams, to make it grow any kind of crops.

We rode along steadily for about six hours, till we came to where the ferry boat ought to be, but as usually happens on these occasions, it was on the other side of the river.

The Ili river about here varies in width from 200 to 400 yards at this time of year, and owing to the melting snow the current was very swift and the water extremely muddy. After much delay the ferry boat crossed over, but it needed the services of five horses on the bank to tow it up to the spot that it had originally left, as during the last crossing, it had drifted over half a mile down stream.

At length, after much talking and shouting, all the luggage was put on board and some of the ponies as well, others were driven into the water and made to swim over by themselves, while others were attached to the sides of the boat in order by swimming to help to tow the boat across.

Just as we were ready to start one of the ponies broke loose and one of the men had to gallop after him to catch him. This operation took fully an hour, by which time a dense black line of cloud and dust appeared, stretching across the valley and approaching at the rate of an express train. This kind of storm is called by the people here a "buran" or "shimal" and they are fairly frequent at this time of year. Everyone now wrapped themselves up in their coats and cowered at the bottom of the boat.

The air was full of sand: every landmark was blotted out and the river rose in great waves. This storm continued until dark and as the ferry was unable to cross while it lasted, we were compelled to camp on an island about eighteen inches above the water, which was the highest piece of land close by, and with the river rising steadily. With the greatest difficulty, the smallest tent was put up, and I retired in it to sleep with a bad headache from the heat of the sun.

Shortly afterwards everyone else took refuge in it, as a deluge began which lasted all night, and by morning our island was barely an inch above the water level.

The morning luckily broke fine and clear. The air was much crisper and there was fresh snow on the higher mountains. By 6.30 a.m. the river was crossed without any further trouble, the boat being carried over partly by the current, and partly by being towed by the horses swimming on either side. There was then a long stretch of flat country to be crossed, dotted over with villages and crops, until we came to the mountain range which separated the Ili valley from the Tekes valley. Here the track followed the small valley of the Su-assu (the river-road). At times the way lay through pretty little gorges, with bushes of yellow and white roses and wild apricot trees on either side. Willow trees lined the banks of the little stream and at times high rocky cliffs rose up on either side of the path. Wild geraniums, spiraeas, aquilegias and an extremely pretty campanula abounded. This campanula was almost white with blue veins in it and a deep black and orange centre. There was a wild garlic too which had very little smell, and which was of a lovely blue hue, like a miniature agapanthus.

We stopped about five o'clock that evening and pitched camp in a small meadow close to the stream, after a march of some twenty-two miles and a climb of 2,500 feet. We were now nearly at six thousand feet in height and the temperature had become pleasantly cool. Just after dark the usual thunder-clouds rolled up, but the storm today missed our valley.

The following morning we were off by seven o'clock. There was such a delightful fresh feeling in the air and the ride up this narrow valley was delicious. The track kept crossing and recrossing the little rushing torrent and as we mounted steadily higher, tall dark spruce firs (*Picea schrenkiana*) appeared on either side. They were taller and thinner in appearance than the European variety and with rather longer needles: among them were many mountain ash trees (*Sorbus tianschanica*) in full flower. Their flowers are larger than the Scotch mountain ash and they formed a very pretty contrast to the dark fir trees.

Several different kinds of clematis hung down from the trees, wild roses, white, yellow and orange in colour, were dotted along the banks of the stream, spiraeas, purple monkshood, yellow and orange poppies, campanulas and hundreds of other flowers abounded.

The track now rose very steeply to the top of the pass (8,500 feet), where we had a magnificent view looking backwards across the Ili valley to Kuldja and the snow mountains to the north of

Kuldja. To the south the view extended over the wide Tekes valley across to the main chain of the Tian Shan mountains. To the south-west towered up an immense snowy chain of peaks, many of whose summits must have been over 20,000 feet in height. It was a glorious day with the air so fresh and clear, and with not a cloud to be seen anywhere, that it seemed most unlikely that within a few hours the rain would be coming down in torrents, so sudden are the changes of weather in these mountains.

Close to the summit of the pass, we overtook many Kirghiz, who had just come from Russian territory and were seeking new pasture lands in China. The settlements of moujiks in Semiretchinsk are gradually driving the nomad inhabitants of Russian territory over the Chinese border. These had all their worldly goods and tents carried on the backs of bullocks, who did not enjoy the steep climb up to the top of the pass. Men, women and children were all mounted on their wiry little ponies, the children looking most picturesque in their big fur caps, yet quite capable, even the smallest ones, of looking after large herds.

On the south side of the pass the slopes were very much more gentle, and the track led through meadows of the greenest and most luxuriant grass, in places carpeted with deep blue forget-me-nots, marsh marigolds and pansies of all shades. Fir trees and willows grew in the valleys and rushing streams seemed to be everywhere. This pleasant zone lasted for some nine miles until we came to the foothills. Here the hills were low and though covered with grass, there were no trees to be found now and the sun became hotter and hotter. My face already burnt by the hot sun of the last two days grew very painful and it was a great relief when a cloud veiled the sun.

On the way we passed numerous chukar (*Caccabis chukar*), snow pigeons, the ordinary blue rock pigeons and many marmots. I also saw a couple of Brahminy duck which breed in the marshy spots high up in these mountains. Immense herds of horses were everywhere grazing and getting fat on the luscious grass, for the wealth of these nomad peoples lies in the number of horses they own.

In the afternoon Rahmah Khan who was supposed to know the way, lost the track and we went on further than we need have done, but at length at six o'clock after going for over eleven hours and covering about twenty-nine miles, we found a little scrub for firewood and pitched camp at a height of 4,800 feet. Soon after it began to pour with rain and continued all through the night.

We could not start early next morning as the tents were soaking and we had to wait for them to dry. There was much discussion as to which way to go, Rahmah Khan wanting to go one way and I another; as neither of us knew the way, but as I had a map, they followed my suggestion which proved to be the right way. The other track which Rahmah Khan favoured, would have led us many miles astray. From camp there was a steep and slippery climb, after the rain during the night, on to a ridge which separated the camp from the Tekes river.

It was a cloudy morning and not hot which was lucky, as there was no vestige of shade on the way. The chukar were calling all round on the hillside and appeared to be very tame. There was a steep descent to the Tekes river which was crossed by a wooden bridge built on the cantilever principle. It did not appear to be very strong, but was quite sufficiently so for its purpose, as there was no wheeled traffic to go over it. Next month, as it happened, it was washed away for the first time for fifteen years by a big flood that came down from the mountains.

At this time of year the river was quite unfordable, owing to the melting snow, and as this was the only bridge for many miles, there was a constant stream of horsemen crossing over it with flocks of sheep, goats, cows and ponies, moving from the lower pasture grounds in the valley to the higher summer pastures. Everyone that crossed over had to pay a toll for the big flocks the toll was as much as one sheep for every hundred that crossed over.

Along the river banks were bushes of sea-buckthorn, and near there I passed several pheasants, very like our English ones, only with a well defined white ring round their necks. The fields and slopes of these valleys were carpeted with Edelweiss, beyond the dreams of avarice of a German tourist.

Near the Tekes river were some handsome pale pink lilies with a strong musk scent. I collected some seeds from them, but as they were hardly ripe, I fear they will come to nothing.

The track now followed the right bank of the Tekes river for some miles down stream across a hot and treeless grassy plain till we came to a small village on the banks of the Chulak Terek. Here in a small house, lived the Chinese mandarin that was in charge of the Kazaks and Kirghiz of the Tekes valley. I stopped on the way to call on him and found him most friendly and hospitable. He gave me a cup of tea and some sweetmeats, followed afterwards by bowls of koumiss. This latter is mildly fermented mare's milk. I had at first some hesitation in tasting it, but soon found it to be most refreshing and palatable on a hot day. The Kazaks and the Kirghiz are extremely fond of it and in the summer months drink an enormous quantity of it.

The mandarin was a short, rather fat little man, who pretended that he had a great deal of work to do and was always kept busy, especially in keeping the peace between the Kazaks and Kalmucks. The Kalmucks are all Buddhist by religion, while the Kazaks and Kirghiz are all Mohammedans. Last year there was much fighting between the two races over grazing lands and there is always much bad feeling between the two religions.

The little mandarin was much worried by the numbers of Kirghiz that had come over from Russian territory and who had settled down in the Tekes valley: these had all refused to pay taxes saying that they were Russian subjects. He told me that during the last year over a thousand families had come over. The little mandarin presented me as I left with a whip studded with silver, as he saw that mine was broken, and also with a basket of fresh vegetables which were most welcome. He also kindly sent a man off with a letter giving instructions to all the Kazaks and Kirghiz that they were to give us every assistance.

We then rode on for a couple of hours after leaving the Chulak Terek stream and pitched camp just as a bad rainstorm started, after only doing a march of about fifteen miles. A local Kirghiz chief brought me some cream and firewood, with many apologies that he had nothing else to offer as his camp had that day started moving up to their summer pastures and he himself was leaving the following morning. There was more rain during the night and this was followed by a cloudy morning so that the march over this grassy and treeless plateau was quite cool. For the first six miles the path gradually ascended over pleasant grassy downs. The grass everywhere was full of pigeons, hares and marmots. The latter are not as pretty as the Kashmir marmot, as they are much greyer and more uniform in colour.

After rising to a little over 6,000 feet, there was a steep descent of 1,400 feet to the Kok-su river, where it leaves the mountains and comes out into the flat Tekes valley. The river was spanned by a roughly made cantilever bridge, as it was quite unfordable at this time of year and does not become fordable till the month of September. Shortly after crossing the bridge we were joined by a Kirghiz chief and a few of his followers, who accompanied us on the long uphill climb of 2,600 feet in order to get out of the Kok-su valley.

The hunting grounds which we are now making for lie at the head of the Kok-su (Blue water river) valley, but it is quite impossible to go up the valley from the Tekes valley, as huge cliffs come right down to the water on either side and as it is unfordable now, it would not be possible to cross from side to side to try and avoid them. Even in the autumn the lower reaches of the Kok-su are considered impassable, as the water is very deep and only in winter time, when the river is frozen over, is it possible to go right up the valley from the Tekes.

We have therefore to make a great detour parallel to the Kok-su valley and to cross several high passes in order to reach the headwaters of the Kok-su river.

On getting to the top of the pass leading from the Kok-su valley into the Little Kustai valley, it suddenly turned cold and started to hail, so the Kirghiz chief carried me off to one of his auls, which was not far off, and insisted on my stopping there and drinking koumiss until it was all over. He and his followers drank a great deal of it and became very merry in a short while.

Soon afterwards, after a march of only 17 miles, we pitched our camp near the rushing Kustai torrent, at a height of 6,000 feet, among some spruce firs and poplars, and on a grassy lawn covered with wild flowers. Our Kirghiz friend not long afterwards put in an appearance to have a look at the camp and enquired if we would like any fish to eat. On replying that we would like some very much, he sent for his fishing rod, which consisted of a massive pole with a string attached to it, on which were two bullets to act as weights: at the end of the string was a large unbarbed hook. He then got a man to put a worm on to the hook, which he then gently lowered into one of the pools. As soon as he felt a bite, he gave a sharp jerk, which flung line and fish straight on to the bank. In this manner in a very short time he had caught some eight fish, weighing on an average about half a pound each. I do not know to what species the fish belonged: they were undoubtedly bottom feeders as their mouths were underneath and they had two suckers. They were very prettily marked with long curly marks of brown and gold.

I was just about to take a photograph of the fisherman fishing, when he stopped me and asked me to wait a moment. He then hurriedly produced out of his pocket two medals given him by the Chinese Government, which he proceeded to pin on to his breast. He then started fishing again and I was allowed to photograph him. The stream a few minutes after this suddenly turned a bright red colour, as there had been a bad storm higher up the valley, and this put an end to all fishing for that evening.

These Kirghiz are extremely friendly and are most hospitable people: they seemed delighted to see strangers and do everything they can to help them. Shortly afterwards one of his followers produced a sheep, which he insisted on my accepting, saying that I was his guest.

There was a very heavy dew during the night and the tents were soaking, so once again we had to wait for them to dry before we could start. Our friend came round again to say goodbye and to wish us good luck, and brought more koumiss for us to drink. He apologised for having to hurry off before we left, as the Chinese tax collector had arrived and he had much business to do with him.

The track that we followed led us at first up the valley of the Little Kustai, and extremely pretty it was with the rushing river bordered with poplars and fir trees.

Immense forests of these great spruce firs (*Picea schrenkiana*) stretched up on either side of the Valley for thousands of feet, almost up to the snow line. High above the dark woods towered into the blue sky glorious snowy peaks, whiter than ever from the fresh snow that had fallen the last few days. It was one of those perfect summer days that are to be found in the mountains, with scarcely a cloud in the sky, and with the air wonderfully clear, washed clean by the rain of the past week. The earth and the trees and the flowers all smelt so good that life was really worth living. After a while we left the valley of the Little Kustai and climbed on to a lovely plateau between 7,000 and 8,000 feet in height, backed on one side by a chain of snowy peaks, and looking far away on the other side over the broad Tekes valley. The plateau was covered with the most luxuriant herbage and flowers: monkshood and delphiniums grew everywhere. Here were the summer pasturages of the Kazaks and the plateau was dotted all over with their white "auls".

It was interesting to watch the way in which these were put together and set up. The women did all the work. They first fixed together the circular framework of sticks, lattice fashion, and then tied the white felt over them. They were very comfortable and warm inside, and there was plenty of room to stand upright and move about: their shape helped them to withstand the gales, which are frequent, and the covering of felt kept the wind out and the heat inside. Around the walls were arranged many-coloured carpets and blankets, and brilliantly coloured boxes with all their worldly treasures in them. In the centre of the aul would be the fire place and there was a hole in the roof to let out the smoke. Light was admitted through the door and also from the hole in the roof. My guide insisted on taking me to every group of auls that we passed and at every one I had to drink either milk or cream or koumiss. I should not like to say how many bowls of the latter I was forced to drink during the day. They all seemed to think that every European was a doctor, as all the sick were at once produced and I was asked to heal everything from a broken leg to ophthalmia.

The shikari that I wanted to get, Tola Bai by name, lived in their neighbourhood, so we went to pay his camp a visit. He was unfortunately away, shooting wapiti, which at this time of year was a very profitable occupation, as their horns when in velvet could be sold to the Chinese for medicinal purposes at a rate of £10 to £12 for a good head. Tola Bai had never received my letter asking him to meet me, and so knew nothing about our coming, but we saw his wife and took off his two sons with us to camp for the night to make further arrangements.

The path now led up and down through the most beautiful fir woods, many of the trees being over twenty feet in circumference at the base. I measured the height of one fallen monarch, by no means a very large one, and found that it must have been over 165 feet in height. The smaller trees were mostly willows and mountain ash: the latter were now covered with white flowers which threw into relief the dark green of the fir trees. We then came down to a river called the Big Kustai and pitched our camp, after only going thirteen miles, on its banks under some fir trees at a height of 6,700 feet.

We did not do a longer march as we were anxious to hire two more riding ponies, and also to try and secure the services of a shikari until Tola Bai joined us. One of his sons is being sent off tomorrow to fetch him and bring him on to Karagai Tash to join us there.

There was much trouble in procuring the horses we wanted, as their owners said that several times they had not been paid for them, and only last year an Englishman coming from India had never paid them, as his servant a Karhgarian had kept the money that was intended for them. If only people would always pay out the money themselves to whomsoever it was due instead of leaving it to their servants to do, it would save a great deal of unpleasantness afterwards. The local headman arrived soon after we had pitched camp with a skin full of koumiss, and not long afterwards one of Tola Bai's sons arrived with a sheep as a present, so that we have plenty of fresh meat in camp now to last for some time. Here we were able to secure the services of a temporary shikari in one Kulde Beg.

Starting early we forded the Big Kustai river which had a good deal of water in it and then climbed up over grassy meadows some 1,200 feet. Never anywhere in the world have I seen such an abundance and variety of wild flowers as I saw today at heights of between 7,000 and 10,000 feet. We passed first through fields of phloxes and Japanese anemones – the latter were I imagine a species of Ranunculus, but very like what we call Japanese anemones in English gardens – then appeared quantities of dark red snapdragons, a beautiful blue flax, golden marsh marigolds, great yellow poppies, sweet scented aquilegias and hundreds of other flowers besides. At the lower heights between six and eight thousand feet, white and yellow were the predominating colours on the hillsides, but between eight and ten thousand feet blues and purples seemed to take the place of white.

After crossing two or three small valleys, we came to several auls where the owners insisted on giving us tea. Here we managed to secure another riding pony.

The ordinary pack-pony is not much use for riding among the precipitous slopes of the Tian Shan valleys; they are not sure-footed enough and ponies accustomed to the steep hillsides are a necessity for this purpose. It is only a very sure-footed pony that will not come to grief on some of the awful slopes that have often to be crossed in a day's shooting.

It was necessary also to have several riding ponies as it would have been cruelty to animals to ride the same pony every day out shooting, when the start was made before dawn and the return was often not till after dark.

These mountain ponies that we hired at these camps, turned out to be really excellent beasts, with no vices, very hardy, wanting no food beyond the grass that grew everywhere and extraordinarily sure-footed and full of intelligence. I was riding today one of the new ponies that I had hired yesterday: he was a chestnut and really an excellent beast. He was very fat and though the march was a trying one with a lot of uphill climbing, he went well and shewed but few signs of fatigue at the end of the day.

After leaving the auls, we climbed up steadily through glorious forests to the grassy meadows at the edge of the tree line which is here a little over 10,000 feet. The grass now became shorter, but was full of iris and primulas and some quite new varieties of flowers appeared. The most astonishing flowers of all were the pansies, white, yellow, blue and every shade of colour up to deep purple and quite as large as any that are found in gardens at home. For

88

miles the hillsides were a variegated carpet of these pansies, and so close together did they grow that every step we took crushed some of them: it was impossible to avoid doing so. Never anywhere else have I seen such a luxuriant flora. The flowers in Kashmir were very wonderful, but these here were still more so. Every flower that is grown in our English or Irish gardens seemed to be represented on these slopes. The weather again today was glorious, and throughout the march there were superb views of distant snowy chains, stretching from far beyond Kuldja, past the headwaters of the Kash river and on in a great semicircle towards Manass. Every detail in this wonderfully clean atmosphere stood out clear and distinct. During the course of the afternoon a roe-deer suddenly got up in front of the ponies, but his horns were still in velvet: we also saw many tracks of wapiti.

In places the ground was very swampy and several times over we only narrowly escaped being bogged. Towards evening after a march of some twenty miles, we dropped down into the pretty Kurdai valley where we camped under some fir trees near the river at a height of 8,700 feet. There was plenty of dry wood about, so we were able to make a roaring camp fire, as the wind was very keen.

The next morning we did not start till 8.30 a.m. as the weather early was unsettled and it was snowing higher up in the mountains. However, as it partially cleared and the sun came out, we decided to make a start and try and cross over the Kurdai pass into the head of the Jirgalan valley. The Russian map marked the Kurdai pass as only 6,700 feet in height, but as we were already over 8,000 feet, I knew this must be a mistake, but imagined that the six was probably a misprint for nine, and that the height of the pass would be about 9,700 feet and so did not trouble to put on warmer clothes. Little did I guess that the height of the pass was nearly 13,000 feet.

The path led up the Kurdai valley, at first passing through fir woods and then over grassy meadows. As we got higher, the grass became shorter and the ground was carpeted with a handsome primula, having long petals of a deep carmine colour and with a white centre. Wherever the snow had just melted, there grew a double anemone, with a bright yellow centre whose petals varied in colour from white to the bluey green of the ice in a deep crevasse. At 12,000 feet the ground free from snow was covered with these primulas and anemones which seemed to mind neither the frost nor the snow.

The fine weather of the past two days unfortunately did not last, and after we had gone a short distance, it began to drizzle and this soon turned to snow as we got higher. The snowfall of the previous winter had been unusually heavy in the mountains and much of this had not yet melted, with the result that the last five or six hundred feet of climb was in deep soft snow. This was very trying for the ponies who kept sinking up to their bellies in it. At one place there was an ice slope covered with fresh snow on which we and all the ponies slipped and slid down a considerable distance, luckily without any danger whatever, as the slope was not steep, but it took us a long time before we could get across this ice slide.

All this time the snow was coming down steadily and there was a thick fog so that it was impossible to see more than thirty or forty yards in any direction.

It was with quite a feeling of relief that I arrived at the top of the pass, thinking that now all our difficulties would be over, but on going ahead to start to go down I suddenly found myself brought up short by an enormous snow cornice fully twenty-five feet in depth, down which there appeared to be no way. At first it looked as though we should have to turn back, but sending Kulde Beg in one direction and going myself in the other, we eventually managed to find a place that looked passable. I managed to get down all right and my riding pony, but when it came to the first laden pony, he sank so deep in the snow, as to be almost buried and then made no attempt whatever to move. The load had then to be taken off and the pony dug out and made to slide the remainder of the way down the slope. This process had to be repeated with all the ponies so that it was not till after five o'clock in the evening that we got out of this deep snow. By this time in my thin summer clothes I was bitterly cold and soaked through from the deep snow in which I had been floundering when trying to extricate the horses. The snow now came down with renewed energy and the ground below the snow line soon became white and very slippery, but pushing on as fast as we could, at last after eight o'clock we reached the first trees and there pitched a very wet camp in long soaking grass at a height of 9,600 feet. We were now at the head of the Jirgalan valley, having covered during the day's march about twenty miles.

The following morning, July 1st, was spent in drying all our wet clothes. John, who had been carrying my big camera the day before, had left it in the snow at the top of the Kurdai pass when we were unloading the ponies in the deep snow, so Kulde Beg was sent back to try and find it. This he was lucky enough to do, in spite of its being buried under several inches of new snow that had fallen during the night. Fortunately the camera was none the worse for its exposure.

During the morning, besides drying all the wet clothes, we had to collect enough wood for the next three days, as there was none to be got at the next camp. We did not therefore attempt to move till after mid-day.

We were now making for the headwaters of the Kok-su and the Yulduz Plains along the edges of which were the feeding grounds of the wild sheep (*Ovis ammon karelini*). Once over the Sarytin pass we were on ground where the wild sheep might be met at any time.

We now went up a small side valley of the Jirgalan valley which led up to the Sarytin pass. At first we rode across grassy meadows carpeted with pansies, then as we got higher, primulas and anemones took the place of the pansies almost to the top of the pass. This pass, though 12,600 feet in height, was not nearly so difficult as the Kurdai pass owing to the slopes being far more gentle. Its chief difficulty was the bogginess of the ground and the way had to be picked out with great care. On the far side of the pass, there was a tiresome piece of soft snow to be crossed, but once that was over the difficulties were passed. On the top of the pass it started to snow and the wind was very cold, but today I had warmer clothes on and so did not feel the cold so much.

On the further side of the pass the slopes were covered with short grass with patches of snow here and there. Beyond was a great plateau extending as far as the eye could see, with gently rounded hills. This was the great Yulduz Plain where we might expect to find the wild sheep.

After going about ten miles, we pitched camp near a large marmot burrow. The only other signs of life about were the ram chukar (snow cock), whose melancholy cries were heard every now and then. There was no wood to be found near the camp, as it was just over 11,000 feet in height and so above the tree line.

We had at last arrived at our hunting grounds after six weeks of most interesting travel by rail, steamer, tarantass and pony.

6

The Wild Sheep of the Tian Shan

The *Ovis ammon karelini*, the wild sheep that live on the Yulduz Plains and near the headwaters of the Kok-su and Agias valleys are an intermediate race between the *Ovis ammon* of the Altai and the *Ovis poli* of the Pamirs. The horns of the *Ovis karelini* are not as long as those of the *Ovis poli*, though they are rather thicker at the base; on the other hand they are not as massive as those of the *Ovis ammon* and instead of being white are a greyish green colour and very deeply ribbed and wrinkled. But they are among the largest of the sheep family in size, the height at the shoulders reaching to about four feet. In colour their coat in winter is rufous rather than grey, with a yellowish ruff round the neck and a white muzzle. The maximum length of the horns ranges from 55 to 58 inches with a girth of 17 to 18 inches.

Their eyesight is extraordinarily good: they will pick up any strange moving object at once, though it may be miles away, and once they have seen anything suspicious, they do not wait, but move off at once and, if frightened, will go for several miles without stopping. Their sense of smell too is very highly developed, and the slightest taint in the wind will make them restless.

They are accustomed to feed early in the morning and continue grazing till towards nine o'clock, when they would lie down and rest for half an hour or so: after this they would get up and move off elsewhere, and then lie down again, repeating this manoeuvre two or three times, until it would be time for them to start their afternoon's grazing. They always gave one the impression of being very restless animals, and when lying down were most difficult to see, as they would choose either a little hollow or else would lie among stones and rocks that exactly matched the colour of their coat. Their homes were on the grassy slopes above the tree line, in places where the mountains were less rugged and precipitous and in the Kok-su valley. They seldom went below 10,000 feet. They were sometimes to be found on the grassy moraines just below the glaciers, and at times even on the glaciers and snow when trying to avoid the attention of the blood-sucking horse-flies.

In the summer and autumn when there was an abundance of rich grass, they grew very fat: on some of the slopes facing south where water was scarce, they used to feed a great deal on the wild garlic which grew everywhere and which quenched their thirst, enabling them to go for a long time without water. It was often a mystery to me how they managed to survive the rigorous winter when the snow lay deep everywhere on the ground, but by cross-questioning Tola Bai and other natives I found out that on the Yulding Plains there was usually a very strong wind blowing, which blew most of the snow off the tops of the rounded hills, and which thus enabled the sheep to get at a little scanty grass. They also managed to find a certain amount of dry grass on the steep slopes that faced south, where the snow either melted very rapidly or else slipped down in the form of avalanches. There were also places in the Kok-su valley where the snowfall in winter was very light, as all the snow was apparently caught on the surrounding mountains and very little fell at the bottom of the valley.

In some winters when the snowfall was exceptionally heavy the sheep would grow weak and thin from want of sufficient grass, and the larger rams would then not have strength enough to support the weight of their massive horns and would lie down and die of weakness. I have often found the heads of large rams lying near exposed hill tops, where they must have in vain tried to scratch the snow away to get at the grass underneath and then unable to do this have perished from weakness.

The first camp that I had when hunting these sheep was at Sary Tur at a height of 11,000 feet, where we arrived on July 1st. The country around was nowhere precipitous, but consisted of great rounded hills and undulating boggy pastures.

The following morning we awoke to find 8 inches of snow on the ground, and the snow coming down steadily; about mid-day it stopped and though the sun was not visible owing to the thick mist, it became really hot for a while, with an intolerable glare, which even coloured glasses were unable to prevent. I wandered out to try and stalk a marmot, but they were very wary and would not allow me within 130 yards of them. At sunset the weather cleared up and the mountains had that clear cold bluey look that often comes in winter. What the cold must be like here in winter, if it is as cold as this in July, I cannot imagine: yet the Kalmucks come up here with their herds in the winter months, as they say that very little snow falls then and grass is always to be found.

Tomorrow, snow or no snow, we must move on down to Karagai Tash, as the supply of wood that was brought with us has been exhausted. The night turned bitterly cold and my sponge inside the tent was frozen solid and the water had ice an inch thick upon it in the morning. Soon after five I started off with Kulde Beg, leaving the pack ponies to follow on later: it was not long before we got into the sunshine which rapidly warmed us up, but as we rose higher the snow got deeper and the glare in the brilliant light became very trying.

The views of the mighty peaks to the south of the Kok-su in their fresh white garb were magnificent, and Karagai Tash and the Yulding Plains were white as far as the eye could see, and a more wintry landscape I have seldom seen in July . . .

We then rode on down to where the new camp was to be pitched in a grassy valley at the foot of the Karagai Tash and the pack ponies arrived shortly afterwards. The height of this camp is only 10,000 feet and by the evening the snow had all melted there. Towards dusk a red wolf approached the camp, but made off before I could get my rifle.

From the camp we have a very fine view of the Karagai Tash or Stone Fir Trees. They are so called because of the likeness of these huge stone pinnacles to trees in the distance. They are a conglomerate formation which has been carved by the weather into every kind of buttress and tower: these are often hundreds of feet high and only fifteen to twenty feet thick and from a distance have a most curious appearance especially when there is snow lying on the ground.

In spite of being at a lower elevation, there was a very sharp frost during the night and the ground was white with hoar frost in the morning. This, however, ushered in a perfect day. We started off up the valley at 5 a.m. and soon rose high up on the grassy hills. The views to the south of the Kok-su were superb, forming an immense chain of great rocky peaks covered with fresh snow, whose precipices descended thousands of feet sheer down into the valleys and whose glaciers sparkled here and there in the brilliantly clear atmosphere. After going a little way we spotted a small ram and some ewes, which we watched for a while, but finding that there were no others with them, they were left undisturbed.

We also saw a small animal which the natives called a "borse": it looked rather like a badger, something between a badger and an otter, and about twice the size of a marmot. It was grey in colour with very long fur and a big broad tail. We gave chase and very nearly caught it, but just as we were on to him, he disappeared into a hole.

The grass here was still rather brown and dried up, and there were not many flowers to be seen, only a few primulae, anemones and pansies here and there. The day was a very hot one and the sun caused another skin to peel off my face and made it very sore. In the afternoon we wandered under the Karagai Tash and a most curious formation they were when seen from close. It seemed as though we were wandering among the ruins of some great fortress built by the giants of old, so human did some of these walls and ramparts appear. Every pebble in these conglomerate towers was rounded, so that it is probable that the whole of this place was at one time under water. Among these towers we came across a herd of about twenty ibex, but as there was no large head among them, we did not disturb them more than possible. Soon afterwards, just below the Karagai Tash, we saw a large flock of some seventy wild ewes and lambs. These we watched for some time as they were such a pretty sight, playing and frolicking about not a hundred

ea house in Kuldja.

ward-Bury inspects the penny bus from Kuldja to Suidum.

The laiden tarantasses stop at some Kazak tombs.

A ferry across the busy Ili river.

A precarious crossing on the Tekes river.

mad women setting up their auls.

hing in the Kustai river.

In the Karag.
Tash.

Snow on the
plains in July

The view from
a bivouac in
the Alpes
Ochak.

of the author's favourite photographs of the Alpine-style scenery below heights, where he revelled in the wild flowers.

Akbulak pass.

The view above Kinsu.

Campsite at Karagai Tash.

view from Eagles' Nest Camp.

gles' Nest Camp, Kembulak.

In the East Mustamas mountains. Akbulak lake.

The headwaters of the Kok-su.

yards from us and quite unconscious of any human presence. As there was nothing to shoot, we returned to camp, getting badly bogged on the way back.

On arrival there we found that Tola Bai and his son had just arrived. I was very glad to see them as Kulde Beg is not much good as a hunter. Tola Bai was found by his son without much difficulty: as he had only managed to shoot one wapiti, he was very pleased to come to us. He had taken a very short time to come here, for it is remarkable what long distances these Kazaks on their sturdy ponies will cover in one day.

Tola Bai was a curious and interesting character. In appearance he was short and thick set, nearly bald, but with a large and rather ragged brown beard and whiskers. He always used to stoop, and that characteristic together with the hair on his face gave him the nickname of "Agu" or "bear" and at times he really was very like a bear. As I got to know him better I grew after a time quite fond of him and found him to be a first-class hunter. His knowledge of the country and of the ways in all the countless valleys of the Kok-su was perfectly marvellous: where he had been once, he could always find his way again. His eye for country too was extraordinary and, time after time, after a very long detour, possibly over a couple of miles or more of very intricate country, and when I would think we were a long way off our quarry, we would find ourselves not a hundred yards away from the herd that we were stalking. He was extremely quick in spotting wapiti, ibex, roe-deer and bear, as he was accustomed to shoot them himself. After sheep he was not so good and I often used to see them first, when it was already too late to be of any good.

That evening I watched from my tent through glasses a big red wolf hunting some wild ewes and lambs: they out-distanced the wolf every time and I do not think that he managed to catch one, though he was very persevering, but he kept them well on the move all the time.

The next day was wet following a mild night. It was drizzling when we started out and as we got higher, the rain turned to snow. We had not gone far when Tola Bai spied a ram which he said was a big one. Approaching cautiously, I could just make out through

97

the snow that he had horns and taking the shikari's word for it that he was a big gulja (ram) I fired, and he moved off slowly, badly hit. It needed a couple more shots to finish him off, and when I got up to him I found to my disgust that he was only a small one. I was very angry with Tola Bai over this, but his excuse was that we should have no luck if I did not shoot something the first day he came out with me and, as he knew I would not shoot a small one, he told me that it was a big head.

Diary, July 7th
On our camping ground I collected a great bunch of wild rhubarb which I had for supper and excellent it was.

On July 10th we moved camp still lower down into the Kinsu valley: on the way there we saw several roe-deer, two large herds of ibex and a ten-pointer wapiti with his horns still in velvet, which old Tola Bai would have very much liked me to have shot. We also saw a few small rams and ewes, when descending into the Kinsu valley where we pitched camp in a heavy rainstorm at a height of 9,400 feet and after having marched fifteen miles.

We remained in this camp till July 14th. There were plenty of ibex on the mountain sides, also roe-deer and wolves, but as we could see no trace of sheep, we determined to move camp again up towards the source of the Kok-su.

On July 17th we moved about ten miles up the Kok-su and pitched camp not far off its source at a height of 10,800 feet. The weather continued very unsettled with constant thunderstorms and heavy rain. Sitting outside my tent, I saw six rams on the hill just behind the camp. We at once started off to stalk these, and approached within 50 yards of the rams, getting a most excellent view of them. Finding that none of the heads were over forty inches, I left them in peace and bitterly reproached myself for not having brought the camera out with me. Before we got back to camp, the rain came down again in torrents. The country round this camp was very different to what it was lower down the Kok-su. It was much more open and the tops of the hills were much more rounded. Behind the camp the ground rose steeply for about 1,000 feet, and then stretched in a great marshy plain for many miles. This was the edge of the great Yulding Plateau. To the south of the Kok-su river grassy spurs rose up for about three thousand feet and above them were the glaciers and snowy peaks.

The ground for sheep here was unlimited and almost every day it was possible to seek out a new stretch of country.

Our first day from this camp proved to be a most unlucky one. We started off at 5 a.m. up on to the Yulding Plains, where we soon saw a flock of twenty rams, but after examining these carefully with the telescope, we found that there was nothing worth shooting among them. Going on we soon afterwards saw two very big rams lying down about 1,000 feet below us, but instead of going after them at once, Tola Bai wanted first to go to the top of the nearest ridge and look over, as he said that the slopes on the other side were a very favourite haunt for sheep. We looked over the ridge and saw no signs of sheep there, only a very wonderful view over the Yulding Plains, which stretched as far as the eye could see on one side, while behind were mile upon mile of great snowy peaks that extended along the south of the Kok-su valley. We then rode carelessly back down the hill, intending to stalk the two big rams. These had meanwhile got up and moved up the hill, not intending to wait for us. I was the first to see them standing and staring at us not 400 yards away while we were still riding. We then had the pleasure of watching these two rams galloping away without a stop over the plain for at least three miles and when they finally vanished out of sight, they were going quite as fast as when they started. This experience taught us that if ever we saw large rams lying down, to go after them at once, as they seldom remained lying down for long in any one place.

The next day on starting out we crossed to the south side of the Kok-su and climbed up the gentle grassy slopes that led to the glaciers and snowy peaks. On the way we looked down into many small nullahs near the sources of the Kok-su, where we saw several roe-deer, and on the far side of a big valley there was a large herd of ibex with one very good head in it. We, however, left them alone and wandered along just below the snow line, where though there was only a little grass, yet the ground was carpeted with a dwarf ranunculus which made the slopes quite yellow. We presently saw a flock of ewes and were keeping well above them when we suddenly saw ten or twelve rams lying down among some rocks. We hurriedly got under cover and then stalked them immediately, for these sheep are restless beggars and never seem to rest long in one place. I had marked down one big ram lying apart from the others, but when we had got close up to them, they had all moved and were looking suspiciously about them. Picking out the best among the crowd, I fired and hit him badly. Thinking that he would not go far, I fired at a second as he was galloping off and slightly wounded him. Both, however, went off at a good pace uphill and I fired several more shots at them as they went away with apparently no effect. At last finding that I had only one shot left, I kept this and sending Tola Bai back for the ponies, I started to follow up one of the wounded rams. The blood tracks were copious and quite easy to follow over the hill, but on looking over the far side, I and the ram saw each other simultaneously and without waiting a second he sprang off downhill. This happened again a second time, so I then tried to cut him off but he totally disappeared. Tola Bai meanwhile had arrived with the ponies and we slowly followed up his tracks and finally discovered him lying down under a rock and very sick. My last shot then finished him off. It is extraordinary what vitality these sheep have: this one had five bullets in him from a .350 Mauser, his insides were smashed to pieces, yet he could still go on. This one was a fairly old ram and had a nice head of 53 inches.

It was too late now to follow the other wounded ram, as he had gone high up over the snow, so we returned to camp, but before we could get there, we were caught in a bad hailstorm.

There was heavy rain and a gale in the night and fresh snow was lying down to 12,000 feet. Starting off soon after 5 a.m. we crossed the Kok-su and climbed up to where we had last seen the wounded ram yesterday at a height of about 13,500 feet. The glare on the fresh snow was so bad that we had to wear glasses, and the old tracks of the ram were of course covered by the fresh snow. We however suddenly saw him on a moraine below a big glacier and he saw us at the same time. The ram then promptly tried to cross the glacier which was about three quarters of a mile wide and got half way across it, but the snow was so soft that he had to come back. We watched him through glasses floundering about in it, at one time almost buried, at another extricating himself with a great leap, but eventually he managed to make his way into the next valley. Leaving the horses to follow later, we scrambled down some cliffs into the first valley and round into the second one, when we suddenly saw our friend the ram walking across the snout of another glacier. Hurrying on as fast as we could we tried to catch him up, but he had meanwhile moved up along the edge of the glacier and was out of sight. We followed along on his tracks, climbing slowly up a precipitous ridge of rock that divided the glaciers from one another. Every moment we fully expected to come across him: at last we caught a glimpse of him about 400 yards away still going on slowly. He then made several attempts to get out on to the glacier, but the snow was too soft and every time he was forced to come back to the rocks, and as the cliffs hemmed him in on the other side, we thought we were bound to come up with him before long. We kept up the pursuit strenuously till at length finding no more tracks in the snow, with much difficulty and with some hard rock climbing we nearly reached the top of the ridge, when we just saw his head peeping over the top to say goodbye to us, after which he disappeared and slid down a steep snow slope on the far side. By now we had climbed up to a height of 14,500 feet and it was a revelation to me that a heavy animal like the Karelini, accustomed to gentle grassy slopes, could move over really bad ibex ground such as this was. The ram finally disappeared in the direction of Mustamas where I hope he will live for many a day, as he was only very slightly wounded.

I had thoroughly enjoyed this day, which was a most interesting one, as we were up among four or five glaciers the whole time and with grand views all around, and the chase had been most exciting.

[The following morning] we found a curious thistle that looked like a great cabbage in the distance, as the actual flower was surrounded by a great bowl of very pale green and almost transparent and sweet scented leaves.

Diary, July 24th

As the rain was pattering down on the tent when I awoke, I turned over and went to sleep again and did not get up till very late. It continued raining on and off all day, a warm mild rain and the clouds hung low. At one time I thought of going out for a while, but to my surprise and joy, Ismail appeared back from Kuldja with my letters and papers, a day earlier than he was expected. As he brought a large budget, I spent the rest of the day reading letters and papers: he also brought a consignment of beetroot, new potatoes, cucumbers and carrots from the father which are most welcome. He only took seven days to come here from Kuldja and how he found us was a marvel, for he had to track us down here. Letters from India take two months to reach here and I have several invitations to dinners and dances in London last month.

Besides the ordinary blue gentian, there is a curious white variety of it coming into flower everywhere, which seems to be rather later ... The morning turned out very hot with a curious heat haze everywhere.

The changes of temperature in this part of the world are very sudden, and about one o'clock a bitter wind arose which blew with the force of a gale: this was followed shortly afterwards by a terrific hail and thunderstorm. The hail blown with the force of the gale was very painful, and we all cowered on the ground, wrapped up in blankets, till it was over, as at the time we were on the top of an exposed ridge 13,000 feet above the sea. The lightning and thunder were instantaneous, and there was a queer crackling sound in the air which I did not enjoy. The storm luckily did not last long, but we had a long and very wet ride back to camp.

Diary, July 26th

I am afraid the poor little bear is very ill. Yesterday his head was swollen on one side, which I put down to a sting, or to his digging out aconite roots, but this evening his eyes were closed and his head terribly swollen. On looking carefully I found an awful abscess in the roof of his mouth. I cleansed it as far as I could but I am afraid the poison has spread all though his head.

Diary, July 27th
The bear was slightly better in the morning and he had one eye
open.

The following day we crossed to the far side of the Kok-su, much
swollen by the rain in the night, and then climbed up the gentle
grassy slopes to the snow line. Here we rode along just below the
snow as far as the Mustamas valley, but saw nothing, so descending
a thousand feet we came back on a lower level. The flowers on the
hillsides here were very beautiful, some valleys were golden with
poppies, while higher up many coloured pansies, carmine primulas,
anemones, buttercups and daisies orange-red and mauve in colour,
simply carpeted the ground. On the lower level we saw a large herd
of ibex and then some rams. These latter we watched for some
time, but they were on the far side of a valley and while we were
crossing this they had moved lower down. While trying to stalk
them, we ran into some more rams, but these luckily went off in
the opposite direction. We now managed to get quite close to them
as they lay in a little hollow, and I could see all of them with the
exception of the largest one. While leaning over to try and locate
the position of the big ram, a small one saw me, gave a whistle, and
without a second's pause the whole lot galloped off downhill as far
as they could go. I fired at the big one as he disappeared, but
missed him. We then wandered slowly back to the ponies that had
been left at the top of the hill. Here we sat talking for a few minutes,
when casually looking through the telescope to see how far the
rams had gone, to our surprise we found that they had started
feeding on the opposite side of the valley: so after watching them
for some while and finding that they were remaining in the same
place, we thought we would try and stalk them again, though it was
already getting late and they were in the opposite direction to camp.
We crossed the valley that separated us as fast as we could, and on
getting within range found them still feeding in the same place.
This time I managed to get a good shot in at the big one: he moved
off slowly but a couple more shots brought him down and by the
time we got up to him he was dead. He was a very old beast with
a massive head, and though his horns were very much broken, they

measured 55 inches. We then had a very long ride back to camp, but we did not mind this as we were very happy and contented with the results of the day. It was quite dark by the time we got down to the Kok-su, which we only just managed to cross, as the day had been fine and hot, and it was in flood from the melting snow. The manner in which the ponies managed to find their way along the hillsides in the dark without a stumble or a slip was perfectly marvellous and eventually camp was reached after being on the move for sixteen hours.

During the night there was a gale and a bad thunderstorm and the next day was spent in camp. The following morning we decided to shift camp for a few days to a place called Khoja Tash at the head of the Yulduz Plains. On starting there was a curious dust haze everywhere, which had evidently been caused by a big sandstorm in the deserts to the south, for the air was full of dust and the snow had turned quite brown from it. Towards evening under the influence of a strong westerly wind, the haze disappeared and the distance became wonderfully clear.

I started off early with Tola Bai, leaving the baggage ponies to follow on later. We first crossed the Yulduz Plain and then climbed on to the ridge which separated it from the Jirgalan valley. There was a very fine view from the ridge, looking over the Tekes valley and across the broad fields of Ili almost to Kuldja. During the day we saw eighteen rams but they were all small ones. To my surprise we put up a quail when at a height of over 12,000 feet: the wind must, I think, have carried him up there. There were also several families of young ram chukar (snow cock) which we tried to catch, but they were just able to fly and so defeated us. On returning in the evening we found that camp had been pitched in a sheltered spot at a height of 11,700 feet: there was no fuel to be found here so everything had to be brought with us. There were sharp frosts every night that we were in this camp, but the days were beautifully warm and sunny.

The first morning it was found that all the ponies had strayed far away and there was much delay in catching them, so that we did not start till late. We then rode up the valley behind the camp, and soon spied two good rams going up a hill. We started then to go up on the other side, but Tola Bai, like all Kazaks, hated to walk a yard if it were possible to ride and so he rode on to the top of the hill where he met the rams face to face. Before I had time to dismount and fire, the rams had gone off at full speed down the hill and we watched them going on for several miles without stopping.

As the views everywhere were so clear today, I thought it would be a good thing to climb up a rocky peak in the ridge dividing Jirgalan from the Yulduz Plains for the sake of the view. We had to walk, as it was too steep to ride up, but on reaching the summit (13,500 feet) we were amply rewarded. The eye ranged over the Yulduz Plains for some seventy to eighty miles on one side and down the narrow Kok-su valley on the other, where we gazed at over 100 miles of snowy peaks in which without glasses I could count quite fifty glaciers. To the north the eye travelled down the Jirgalan valley and across the Tekes and Ili valleys to the snowy ranges near the sources of the Kash river.

Towards evening we saw five good rams near the Karagai Tash which we left for the morrow. On the way back to camp I caught two young Brahminy ducks which I brought back with me and put in a pool close to camp.

July 31st was another perfect summer's day. We started off to try and find the five rams that we had seen the evening before, but they had completely vanished and we never saw a sign of them all day. Most of the time was spent in wandering among the weird crags and buttresses of Karagai Tash, where we must have seen quite a hundred ibex. The views on all sides of countless snowy peaks and grassy valleys were superb in the brilliant sunshine and clear air. The only fly in the ointment was the horse-flies which were beginning to get troublesome: there were two kinds of them, one like a small bee and the other like a giant house fly, but with a green head. These fastened on to the horses in swarms and also on to one's own neck and hands if not very careful: they had a proboscis like a razor, which drew blood almost immediately: however, their bite did not seem to be poisonous.

In the evening we saw a wolf which we tried to attract nearer to us by calling, but he was too suspicious to approach near enough for a shot.

Diary, July 31st
The little bear is getting ever so much better and today both eyes are open and the swelling is very much diminished.

The next morning we once more rode across the Yulduz Plains: Tola Bai and I went on ahead leaving John and the pack ponies to follow on later. On searching some of the small valleys on the south side of the plain, we only found tracks of wild pig and a few ewes. The wind blew hard all day, but the sun shone brightly and brought out swarms of the green-headed horse-fly which worried us all the time . . .

The pink marguerites and the yellow poppies on the hillsides made a delightful combination when growing together: there was also coming into flower now a very fine deep blue and autumn flowering gentian. The wonderful variety of the flowers was always a source of great joy.

The next day was cloudy which, much to my relief, kept the flies in bed. They only come out when the sun is shining and the moment a cloud passes over the sun, they immediately disappear. We crossed over the Kok-su and climbed high up on the opposite side, up to the snow line. Here there was a grand view of the surrounding country and after searching the ground carefully with the telescope, we made out four rams a couple of miles away in one of the side valleys. From anywhere below they were completely hidden, as they were in a small cup-shaped depression high up on the hillside. Leading the ponies down a most precipitous slope where even they could barely find a footing, we gained the valley. Then followed a long and interesting stalk. Tola Bai had marked down the spot only too well, for he brought me up to within twenty yards of the animals, without our ever having a second glimpse at them. The moment I looked into the little hollow to see if they were still there, they jumped up and went off as fast as possible. I fired at the leading ram just as he was disappearing over the brow and then ran to where I had last seen him, and much to my surprise found him lying stone dead. He had a fair head with horns 51 inches in length and 40 inches from tip to tip. It was very lucky that I had shot this ram, as all the meat in camp had been finished and we should have been reduced to bread and potted meats otherwise. Soon afterwards a snowstorm came on and we returned to camp. The two Brahminy ducks that I had caught the other day are now getting quite tame and are living in a pool of the river close to the camp.

We now decided to move lower down to hunt for ibex, roe-deer and bear, so the following day we moved into the Mustamas valley where we remained till August 20th. Here we were just on the edge of sheep ground, and every now and again came across them.

These wild sheep, the *Ovis karelini*, were without doubt the most difficult animals to approach in the Tian Shan mountains, partly owing to their living in such open country, and partly owing to their restless habits and wonderful eyesight, but a trophy of one of their massive heads was a magnificent reward for all the troubles and hardships undergone in their chase, and the days that were spent in hunting them among the glorious scenery and beautiful flowers of the Tian Shan were among the most pleasant of my recollections.

7

On Ibex

Varieties of ibex are to be found in nearly all the mountainous regions of Asia, occurring throughout the Himalayas, the Tian Shan and the Altai mountains. They are distinguished by the long scimitar-shaped horns that they carry, the front surface of which is boldly marked by well-defined ridges. The maximum length of the horns varies from 55 to 58 inches with a girth of about 12 inches. A distinctive feature in the males is a prominent beard: their coats are of a rough coarse hair, rather inclined to curl and of a brownish colour: the muzzles of the older males are frequently almost white. The females are much smaller animals and of a lighter colour. The height of a full grown male is from 40 to 42 inches at the shoulder.

The ibex of the Tian Shan (*Capra sibirica almasyi*) is in many ways a different animal to his cousin in the Himalayas. He is on the whole a larger beast: his horns are longer and the tips curve more outwards. He also does not carry so strong a smell. As a rule he does not live in such difficult or precipitous country as is found in the Himalayas. In the Tian Shan there are many more grassy slopes and pastures close to the rocks, and on these he is fond of spending the day. They still exist in very large numbers, and in even the smallest nullahs there are to be found herds of a hundred or more ibex. Sometimes I must have come across between 300 and 400 of them in the course of a day. It was frequently the size of the herds that was the chief obstacle to approaching them, as when they were lying down, the herd would be scattered over quite a large area of ground and the biggest heads would always be the ones furthest off. As a rule, however, they were far easier animals to stalk than the wild sheep: their eyesight though keen was not so highly developed and as they seldom took the trouble to look upwards, the easiest way to approach them was from the higher ground. They were not restless like the wild sheep, and when they had once started to lie down for the middle of the day, they stopped there and did not move for several hours, so that there was always plenty of time to arrange a detour in order to get a shot at them. It was a wonderful sight to see a large herd that had been alarmed, streaming away downhill or across the most precipitous spots at full gallop and it was perfectly astonishing how fast they could move on the steepest hillsides. The skin and flesh of the Tian Shan ibex had not that strong and unpleasant goaty smell that the Himalayan ibex had, which made his flesh almost uneatable: on the contrary the meat though sometimes tough, was not bad to eat and I used to live on it for weeks at a time.

In the summer the big herds would be found at heights of from 10,000 to 14,000 feet, the females being nearly always at a lower altitude than the big males. Small herds of females would often be found as low as 8,000 feet on cliffs close to thick woods. In the winter the herds used to come low down into the valleys where the snow would not be so deep and they would then fall an easy prey to the Kazak and Kalmuck hunters who used to feed their camps on them during the cold months. They were too lazy to hunt the ibex in the summer when they were high up on the mountainsides, and when they would have to do a lot of climbing to get near them, but in the winter when the snow had brought them almost to their doors, then they used to hunt them. Their skins they turned into clothes, making either trousers or coats of them, and their flesh they used to dry and eat.

Hunting ibex in this country is a very much easier and less tiring game than it was in Kashmir, as here so much of the country is rideable that all the long and weary climbs uphill are performed on horseback, leaving only the actual stalking to be done on foot. Several times I have ridden up on to a ridge and on dismounting and looking over have found myself within easy range of a good ibex. In the autumn the males used to be very fond of fighting and the clash of their horns could be heard for half a mile and more away. They used to attack one another with great violence, charging with bent heads and each manœuvring to start from the higher ground. The loser in these shock tactics would often be knocked fifteen to twenty feet down hill as the result of a violent blow.

The greater part of July was spent in hunting the wild sheep, but during this month on many occasions ibex were seen and in places where there was no fear of disturbing the sheep, we used to go in pursuit of the ibex. The first herd of ibex that we came across lived among those extraordinary towers and crags that composed Karagai Tash. There were several herds that lived among these towers and who apparently never left them, but as there were no big heads among them, although we frequently saw them, they were left undisturbed.

The next time that we saw any ibex was on moving down the Kok-su valley to a camp in Lower Sary Tur where there were several big herds among which were some quite good heads.

One day after making quite certain that there were no sheep in the neighbourhood, we rode up the valley to the west of Sary Tur, passing at first through a kind of broom that grew like a great club and which was covered with sharp thorns and white flowers. There was a regular forest of this stuff for about a mile: in places it grew about six feet high and was most curious to look at. We then slowly rode on over grassy slopes till we came to the head of the valley which lay at a height of about 12,000 feet. On the side that we had ridden up the slopes were quite gentle, but on the far side were big cliffs and a very steep descent. Dismounting, we crawled to the edge and looked over and saw a fine herd of about fifty ibex not 200 yards away. After watching these for some time and finding that among them were three heads of over 50 inches, I crawled a little nearer and took a careful shot at the one that I thought to be the biggest, only to find that there was a larger one lying hidden under a rock, who at the sound of the shot jumped up and galloped away, and never gave me an opportunity for a shot at him. I was, however, very pleased with the one that I had shot as his horns measured 52 inches.

The views from the spot where the ibex had been lying were magnificent, as we looked straight down into the Kok-su valley many thousand feet below and then across to the giant 20,000-feet peaks of the Agias valley, while in front of us were the mighty crests of the Chalyk Tau, the gleaming ice of whose glaciers showed up against the pure white of the snow and the dark rocky precipices.

A couple of days later on moving camp from Sary Tur to Kinsu, we had to go up the same valley. The weather was unsettled with hail and snowstorms, and during one of the latter we saw a herd of ibex coming down to a more sheltered spot, so Tola Bai and I hurried to meet them as we saw that among them were the two big ibex that had escaped us the other day. Unfortunately by the time that we were within shot, they had also seen or winded us, as the wind was very changeable, and had begun to move off in the opposite direction. Without carefully studying each one through glasses, I could not distinguish which was the biggest head, and there was no time for this, but Tola Bai had spotted our friend at once and kept shouting to me "Kara, kara". Not knowing what "Kara" meant, my mind flew to Hindustani and imagined that he meant one that was standing still, but as they were all standing still at the moment, I was completely puzzled, and before there was time for explanation, the whole herd had disappeared. It was only afterwards that I found out that he meant the darkest one, as "Kara" in Turki means black. This was the second time that this big ibex had eluded us, but six weeks later on meeting him a third time, he fell a victim to the rifle.

In the Kinsu valley, finding that there were no traces of sheep there, we went out after ibex. There were several big herds in the valley and in one of them there must have been over 200 animals. One morning, crossing the Kinsu river by a deepish ford, we climbed up the opposite slopes of the valley. On the way up we heard some wolves howling among the bushes but we could not locate them. By seven o'clock we were at a height of between 12,000 and 13,000 feet, and it was already so hot, that I shed coat, scarf and waistcoat. We sat for a long time on the top of the ridge trying to pick out some ibex, but without success.

The views of the great snowy chain to the south of Koksu were magnificent. We could see a range of snowy peaks of great height for fully 100 miles. Exactly opposite us was a stupendous gorge piercing into the very heart of the chain. Monstrous precipices 5,000 to 7,000 feet towered up on either side with their summits covered in everlasting snow, a most terrifying and awe inspiring vision.

Not seeing any ibex we walked along the ridge and before long saw a herd of some twenty ibex lying down. Creeping along, we approached these with great caution and, picking out the largest one, I fired at him and he disappeared behind some rocks with the others. The herd reappeared again some distance away but he was not among them, so we went down to where he had been lying, but there was no sign of blood anywhere. Suddenly on turning a corner we saw him about 100 yards away wedged in a little cleft under a rock and quite dead. The bullet had gone into him diagonally and had remained under the skin on the far side. His horns were short in height, but had an extraordinary amount of curl in them and measured 53½ inches.

The wild flowers along the ridge were very beautiful, primulas, pansies, anemones, ranunculus were everywhere, and on the ledges and cracks in the rocks a mauve plant flourished belonging either to the campanula or poppy family.

The nights were now getting very cold and the grasses by the streams were covered with icicles every morning, while higher up, it froze in the shade all day.

On August 14th we again rode up the Eastern Mustamas valley and after going a little way saw some ibex in the rocks which we thought might be good ones, and so proceeded after them. The strata here were almost vertical, causing the mountainsides to be most precipitous and to be split up into a number of vertical gullies which were for the most part just passable, but which were apt to be the channels for falling stones all the day long. Leaving the ponies at the bottom of the valley, we climbed up one of these gullies till we were level with the ibex in the next gully and then looked over. There was nothing however worth shooting in the herd, which soon moved off. Two more herds then came up, but there were no big heads in either of them, so we then started to try and climb to the top of the ridge, a climb of nearly 3,000 feet. All the way we kept on disturbing more and more ibex, till the whole mountainside seemed to be alive with herds of small ibex and with the falling stones dislodged by the same. Eventually we saw a big ibex lying down on the top of the ridge and after a long and steep climb up a parallel gully, we got on to the top of the ridge just in time to see him and several others going away as fast as they could across some deep snow, but luckily still within shot. A lucky shot brought down the biggest ibex: his head turned out to be smaller than we had expected, the horns only measuring 50 inches. It was, however, a very handsome head, as the horns had a very wide spread making them appear longer than they really were. We then had a long trudge through deep and soft snow: for part of the way I sat down on the snow and slid along, much to Tola Bai's astonishment who tried to save me, thinking that I was slipping. I had thoroughly enjoyed this day, as there had been plenty of walking and climbing to do: not so Tola Bai, who was always accustomed to ride everywhere. The weather too had been gloriously fine and the views among these giant dolomite mountains were very wonderful and full of lovely colours.

On August 20th we moved camp from Mustamas into the neighbouring valley of Kair Bulak: the pack ponies went the longer and easier way, round by the Kok-su valley, while Tola Bai and I rode over the intervening ridge. The night before had been wet and in the early hours of the morning, the mountains glistened in the bright moonlight under their coating of fresh snow. After leaving the camp, there was a steep ascent of about 3,000 feet: on the way up we saw a good roe-deer, but he made off at once and soon after we rode up to within 100 yards of a herd of ibex that were busy scraping out the grass underneath the fresh snow. I was very sorry that I had not my camera with me as this would have made such a pretty picture, but it had unfortunately gone round with the pack ponies. Snow began to fall now and continued on and off for the next five hours.

At last the mist lifted slightly for half a minute and it was just possible to make out three very big ibex. I fired at one of these and hit him badly, and then fired a second shot at another one as he disappeared in the mist, without any result however. Fearing that they would be lost altogether, I ran down the spur below the clouds, in the hopes of getting another shot, but they were already too far off. There was, however, about 300 yards below us, a large bear standing on his hind legs and looking uphill, full of curiosity to know what all this noise meant. Leaving the shikari to look for the wounded ibex, I ran down after the bear and fired at him, but I am afraid only hit him in the arm, as I was much too much out of breath to shoot steadily. The bear then made off at a great pace round a spur and into some thick bushes where he completely disappeared. By this time I was soaking through and through, what with the snow and the rain and then crawling through the dripping bushes and long grass after the bear, so to get warm I climbed up again to where I had shot the ibex, and found Tola Bai's face wreathed in smiles, and he kept on shouting "Beeg one, beeg one" in the one or two words of broken English that he was beginning to pick up. The ibex certainly was a magnificent beast with horns 58 inches long and 40 inches from tip to tip, with a beautiful curve on them, and was by far the finest ibex that I had ever seen. It was really an extraordinary piece of luck getting him this way in the fog . . .

One day, after losing my knife in the Alpes Ochak valley, I went off by myself to try and find it, and on the way approached quite close to a very fine herd of ibex. There were several among them with horns of over 50 inches, and one of the largest of the herd had only one horn which made him look rather like a unicorn.

On many occasions we had almost unique opportunities for studying the habits of the ibex. One day a large herd of female ibex came within 50 yards of us, as we were sitting down resting. Some of the little ones could hardly have been born a week before, so small were they, but yet they were very lively and full of frolic. One old female had one horn completely twisted round the base of the other which gave her a most curious old maid appearance.

As a rule ibex were very easy animals to approach, and it was seldom too difficult to get within shot of a herd. In some of the valleys where the mountainsides were exceptionally precipitous, it would have been difficult to approach or to shoot an ibex, but the big ibex did not seem to care much for those dangerous valleys and left them generally to the females and young ones. The really big ibex preferred rocks and cliffs that were close to good grazing ground and on these they would usually be found.

In his pursuit we were led into many different kinds of country, and into some of the wildest and most fascinating scenery of the world. To the mountain lover the chief charm of searching for the ibex lay in the fact that they lived amid such wonderful and beautiful surroundings, where every moment was a joy and where every few yards offered a different and more wonderful view of a chain of lofty summits that rivalled in height the mighty peaks of the Himalayas.

The text prepared by the author ends here. For the conclusion of his hunting trip and his return journey to Europe we turn to his diary.

Monday, September 8th

A day of rest in this pretty camp under the birch trees. The weather is heavenly now, hard frosty nights and such glorious sunny days. Ever since the heavy snowfall in the beginning of August it has been delightful. Red and black wild currants abound round the camp so I have plenty of fresh fruit. John says he saw a snipe this morning by the river: I imagine it must have been a snippet or woodcock. The bear is nowadays very happy and he eats every kind of berry except the mountain ash. Tomorrow I hope to go and bivouac for three days up the Akbulak valley: the camp is short of meat, so I shall try and shoot an ibex for them. Thank goodness there are no horse-flies here, either this is too low for them or the frost has killed them at last. I spent the day chiefly in reading and tidying up.

Tuesday–Thursday, September 9th–11th

We started up the Akbulak valley a little before ten, as we were only going about six miles up the valley. The entrance to the valley consists of a narrow rocky gorge and we crossed and recrossed the stream many times picking our way laboriously under the thickest of bushes which here grew up to about fifteen feet in height. They were chiefly willow, birch, poplar and tamarisk, and a few small fir trees. The leaves on the trees are, unfortunately, still very thick and show very little signs of falling at present, though in places they are beginning to turn yellow. This makes the finding of the stag almost impossible as the big ones spend all their day in the bushes and until the leaves fall or the stags start calling, hunting them is almost useless. This year and last year they are exceptionally late in starting calling, possibly this may be due to the abundance of leaves and the summerlike weather that we are having.

After going about four miles the valley widened and we came into pastures of the most luxuriant grass, dotted about with clumps of fir trees and bushes, while high above towering up into the blue sky was a great rocky dome crowned with snow and hanging glaciers. We bivouacked under a clump of fir trees by the side of a small stream: in the afternoon we climbed up into a side valley whence we had a good view in order to see if we could spy any stag. We saw nothing until we had almost got back to camp, when crossing a field two stag trotted out into it and commenced feeding. It was only just light enough with glasses to make out their horns though they were not 300 yards away, but unfortunately, they both proved to be small.

I am having considerable trouble now from the establishment, as they say they have got no meat: they had vast amounts of meat only a little of which they dried, regardless of the morrow: the remainder they partly ate but mostly threw away and now they are perpetually worrying me to shoot something for them so I said I would shoot an ibex. The following morning we, therefore, started up the valley on foot at daybreak, first to see if there were any stag, but after going a couple of miles through the wood and finding one, the horses joined us as we rode up what was evidently partly an enormous old moraine and partly a huge fall of rock from the rocky peaks on either side. This debris had completely filled up the valley to a height of about 700 feet and was the cause of the beautiful lake that we came upon later. After having climbed over this debris we arrived at some flatter and rather marshy ground which at times is under water. Here we saw a bear turning over the stones and after a short and very easy stalk, he succumbed. He had a beautiful coat and was larger than my last bear, though not as large as the first two. Leaving the boy to skin the bear we rode on to a small hill.

At our feet lay the most beautiful lake that I have ever seen: its colour was of the blue of the true old Persian turquoise and surrounding it was a circle of magnificent peaks. Immense cliffs thousands of feet high came steep down into its blue waters. Hanging glaciers in places almost overhung the lake. We rode along the edge of the lake for a while until stopped by cliffs. In shape the lake is a half moon about 2½ to 3 miles in length and from ½ to 1 mile in width: it is evidently very deep and everywhere of this glorious blue. At its head was a magnificent snow peak covered with snow and glaciers.

The lake lies at a height of 11,000 feet and is unmarked on the map. I then thought that I would investigate the first part of the Akbulak pass: the shikari did not want to go and like all natives began to say that it was very far and very difficult: he had only induced me to go round the lake by saying that we could see the pass from there, which of course we could not do. So taking the camera and leaving him behind to look for ibex, I climbed up a big spur which juts into the lake and over which the path has to go as it ends in sheer cliffs down to the lake. This was all over loose stones and bad going, but I was well rewarded when I got to the top of the spur at a height of 12,700 feet. The view was wonderfully grand – how many prachtvolls a German would have used I cannot say. At my feet on either side lay this bluest of blue lakes while opposite was the watershed of the central Tian Shan mountains consisting of a series of snow and rocky peaks of the most fantastic shapes: glaciers and cliffs of ice showing everywhere on their slopes. Opposite me and across the valley lay the Akbulak pass which appears to be about 13,000 feet in height. The last seven hundred feet is a steep slope of loose stones, passable though troublesome for ponies, but free from snow.

I should have gone up to it, but the shikari kept on saying that it was terribly far and impossible to get there in one day (as he would have had to walk a little way and lead the ponies, I discovered), hence the horror of a Kazak at my wishing to go there, which had to be prevented. Immense banks of clouds came rolling up from the deserts and the Tarim basin, possibly monsoon clouds from India, and formed a magnificent background to these snowy peaks.

Photographs, I am afraid, can do it but little justice, though I took many, and my powers of description are feeble.

I told the shikari if he wanted any meat, he must go out and look for an ibex and when he found a herd, I would go and shoot one for him, but he preferred to stop in camp: these Kazaks are too unutterably lazy. While sitting reading in front of my tent, I saw something swimming across the Kok-su, I ran down to see what it was and to my surprise saw it was a wild duck. I watched it come ashore and go under some rocks when I stalked it and pulled it out. It had a damaged wing, but will make a welcome addition to the larder. Most of the day I spent in reading and laughing over *Don Quixote*. Both my cameras keep getting out of order and I fear my photographs will mostly be bad. Tomorrow we move camp a few miles lower down the Kok-su.

Sunday, September 14th

We had a mild warm night and when I awoke it was drizzling, so I did not get up till late. By the time we had packed up camp, it had cleared and we had a beautiful summer's day: showers threatened at times but did not come near us. We crossed the Kok-su twice and pitched camp at the entrance to the Alpes Ochak valley under such a pretty clump of birch trees, mountain ash and fir trees, on the banks of the Kok-su. From my tent I have a lovely view of the great snowy peaks at the head of the Alpes Ochak valley and it is the prettiest camp that I have had. The mountain ash have now turned scarlet and the willows and birch are turning yellow, so I hope the leaves will fall soon.

In the afternoon we rode up through the fir woods to spy for stag and an amusing thing happened to me. I had my khud stick in one hand and with it was busily brushing aside the branches from my face, when without my noticing it we passed between two trees close together and I was brought to a sudden stop by the khud stick catching me in the chest and so tightly wedged between me and the trees that I could not move it. The pony proceeded on slowly and left me suspended in the air in an undignified position without any injury. This place is called the valley of the Sixty Fireplaces because years ago a party of soldiers went through it to Kuchar and in one place built sixty little fireplaces on which to cook their evening meal.

Monday, September 15th

We started off a little before 5 a.m. just when it was getting light to look for the stag that we had seen yesterday. We watched and waited and presently saw a hind move: it was now about 10 a.m. and very hot so Tola Bai went to sleep, while I read *Don Quixote*.

Presently we heard him call, an indescribable sort of sound, something between an escape of steam and a toy pig that can be blown out and then whines as the air comes out of him. We then went down into the valley and cautiously approached the little gully in which we had seen the stag. As we got near we heard a great noise of breaking boughs, but could see nothing at first, because the willow bushes were too thick. However, presently I made out the stag and fired: he disappeared and then went slowly uphill. I fired twice more and then I heard a crash and when we came up, we found him quite dead. He was a ten-pointer, what the head measures, I cannot say until we get it in camp. These stags are enormous animals, as big as a cow and very dark in colour: their skins are very thick. Tola Bai said he would spend the night there cutting him up and that I was to send up ponies to him in the morning. The very first thing he did was to light a fire: he then cut off a huge piece of meat, which he put in the hot ashes for a few minutes and then devoured it.

The postman ought to have been back yesterday with fresh supplies of rice flour and bread, but he has not turned up yet and I do not know what is the matter so that there is starvation in the camp and this supply of fresh meat comes most opportunely.

Tuesday, September 16th

No signs of the postman yet: I cannot think what has happened to him. My servants think there must have been fighting in Kuldja and he is afraid to stir.

Wednesday, September 17th

It was raining early and blowing hard, so that I did not get up till 6 a.m. when it began to clear and we started up the Alpes Ochak valley soon after. During the night the snow came down to within 1,000 feet of camp and it turned much colder. We went a long way up the valley, getting very wet as the vegetation everywhere was very rank and soaking with the two nights' rain. The monkshood was over my head on horseback and the undergrowth consisted chiefly of tamarisk, birch and willow. The leaves are at last beginning to come off the bushes and the mountain ash are in their full scarlet apparel.

There are two very fine snow peaks that must be over 17,000 feet at the head of the Alpes Ochak valley and today with a fresh mantle of snow they looked most imposing. There is an easy pass at the head of this valley across the main chain of the Tian Shan and it leads into the same valley on the other side that the Akbulak pass leads into.

In the afternoon we had a heavy snowstorm for the best part of an hour, during which we took refuge under a rock, and a very cold and long ride home followed. However, a large camp fire and a good cup of tea soon warmed me up again. The moon is nearly full and the nights are beautiful. Still no sign of our postman, so I have sent the boy over the Kustai pass to try and get some flour and rice from the Kazaks.

Thursday, September 18th

The coldest night that we have had so far and the ground everywhere frozen like iron. I did not enjoy riding down the Kok-su valley in the early morning and fording the river three times. My feet of course got wet and I could not get them or my hands warm, as an icy cold wind sprang up but it only lasted luckily for a couple of hours.

The day was a magnificent one, not a cloud anywhere in the sky and the sun has still I am glad to say, considerable power. After going about four miles, to our horror we saw the valley that we were going to spy filled with horses, so that it was useless going there. We went down and persuaded one of the herds to come across the river and talk and he brought the inevitable koumiss of which Tola Bai drank nearly a whole sackful. I did not understand the conversation but on return to camp I found out through John that beside herds and horses there was also a party of hunters in the camp and that they had disturbed and shot in all the nullahs that we were going to visit, especially the next one to this which is the best of all, so that I do not expect now to get another stag. If I can only catch them flagrante delicto, I shall keep their rifles. In the afternoon we went up a side valley near camp, but neither saw nor heard anything. The herds told us that there had been fighting at Kuldja and I am afraid our postman has been scuppered or else is afraid to move. The two head huntsmen of the party are called Chal and Chinabai.

Howard-Bury found himself thwarted by the presence of local huntsmen repeatedly over the next week, despite sending a boy "to tell them to go away".

Monday, September 22nd
The afternoon we spent wandering through the thick forests at the bottom of the valley. We saw a very large bear asleep and tried to stalk him, but the undergrowth was so thick that we came out a few yards below him and he got our wind and with some very angry expressions rushed away in the thick bushes and though not more than fifteen yards away the undergrowth was so thick, I could not get a shot. It now began to rain, which turned to snow before we got to camp and we had an awful uphill climb of 3,000 feet to camp and I was quite exhausted by the time I got back.

The boy had caught the hunters all right, who were Kirghiz from Koktuck and they left the valley at once, but alas all the damage has been done. A wolf gave us a melancholy serenade which exactly expressed my feelings. The hunters informed the boy that there were forty other hunters in the nullahs lower down, so that my last chances of getting another stag are gone.

Howard-Bury eventually stalked and shot "an enormous animal with a very good head" on a wooded hillside at 11,000 feet. The horns were fifty-two inches long and forty-two inches from tip to tip.

Tuesday, September 23rd

A large dead fir tree over 100 feet in height has fallen during our absence within five yards of my tent: I am rather nervous about another one close by. I saw five pelicans on their way south going over the Alpes Ochak pass: we saw some chukar and black partridges near camp. Nearly every day now I kill a snake: it is a wonder they are still above ground in this cold.

Wednesday, September 24th

The colouring and autumn tints in the valleys are very beautiful, the mountain ash and a shrub like a berberis are everywhere scarlet, the willows and the birch are bright yellow and the poplars are quite orange and contrast well with the dark green of the firs, while above are the great snow covered peaks and the deep blue sky. Today was again quite cloudless: this autumn climate is certainly most delightful.

Friday, September 26th

It has taken me nearly five weeks, hunting practically every day to get two stags, so now I can return content to Kuldja. Unless the Chinese can be induced to do something to protect these stags, they will in a few years' time be quite extinct. The Kazak, Kirghiz and Kalmuck hunters go out in parties of from four to nine men, at all times of the year and organise regular drives killing hinds and immature stags or whatever comes their way. I shall do my best to try and induce the Chinese to prohibit stag hunting altogether for a certain number of years, but the central authority is at present so weak, that I fear nothing will be done.

Wednesday–Thursday, October 1st–2nd

We started off at 7.30 a.m. under a very threatening and lowering sky. We had not gone for an hour before it began to snow heavily: just after the snow started we put up a covey of partridge, after which I went. I knocked down three, but only recovered one, as the other two fell among rocks and juniper bushes. The roots of the juniper formed an impenetrable tangle and though we searched for some time in a blinding snowstorm, we could not find them.

The one we picked up, Tola Bai lost later on in crossing the pass. Yesterday he had been telling us that this was a very easy pass and even if a horse fell, he could not hurt himself. We experienced otherwise, for presently we had to cross a very steep slope of shale, hard frozen and with a coating of snow, which was extremely slippery. Half the ponies got over safely, when one of the last string slipped and very nearly dragged four others with him: the rope luckily broke and the pony disappeared from view rolling over and over. After crossing this bad place we came to a spot where we could see down into the valley and there we saw the pony lying motionless in the snow between 500 and 700 feet below the spot where he had fallen, his load scattered all over the place. I left Ashim and Truspec with a couple of ponies to pick up the load while we went on.

A regular blizzard was blowing now and snow had already drifted as deep as one's waist and it did not take five minutes for the snow to cover up our tracks. Tola Bai now proceeded to lose his way. After floundering about for some time in two different directions, I made all the pack ponies stop in a central place near a small lake, as I intended to camp there until it was fine and Tola Bai could find his way. Meanwhile I went back to where I had left the two men and told them that we had lost the way. To my great surprise I found them still with the fallen pony who was actually alive and except for a few cuts none the worse. The snow must have saved him, but they had to bring him a very long way round and could not join us for some time.

When I got back to the other ponies, Tola Bai said that he had found the way to the pass and that we could easily get to bushes on the other side before dark. It was now three o'clock, with about three more hours of daylight and it actually took us over nine hours to get to the bushes.

We reached the top of the Karasir (Black cow) pass about 13,600 feet about four o'clock. The pass is really only a slight depression in the main chain of mountains that divide the Kok-su from the Tekes valley and the view from the summit on a fine day to the south must be very fine, as it is not shut in at the bottom of a valley as most passes are.

It was still snowing and about a foot of fresh snow had fallen and on the north side of the pass, thanks to all the old snow in addition, it lay from three to four feet deep. The snow consisted of the finest powder and was the easiest snow to get through that I have ever experienced.

On reaching the top to my horror I saw a very precipitous descent, covered with big rocks and again Tola Bai did not know the way. He started off leading his pony, but before he had gone many yards he got his pony stuck and none of us could get it to stir. So leaving it there as I did not want all the other ponies lost too, we tried another way down. At every step I floundered and disappeared in the snow and the same with the ponies who kept disappearing in a cloud of fine powdery snow. We got down about 300 feet leaving en route, besides Tola Bai's pony, my gun, bed, table, chair, etc, when we were confronted with a still steeper slope. Here two more boxes went, but luckily just as it got dark, Ashim and Truspec arrived, and we managed to get the ponies down in the dark.

It was impossible to walk a step, it was all big rocks under the snow and one simply slipped and fell. At the bottom it was luckily flat and I made them stop. The snow was between two and three feet deep here but we managed to get up a tent anchoring it to boxes and horns in the snow. The snow had nearly stopped now and it was freezing hard.

I do not think any of us slept much during the night. I certainly did not, though the bear did perhaps. We all went hungry to bed and I was very fearful of half of us being frostbitten in the morning, as during the day everything had got wet and then frozen. Camp at 13,000 feet in deep snow in October is no joke, especially without wood; luckily the night proved much warmer than it might have done, as it was cloudy and a couple more inches of snow fell.

As soon as it was light, the four men went back to rescue the pony and the luggage strewn along the hillside. The pony had alas broken its leg during the night, in its struggles to get free and had to be killed, but the kit was recovered and we then started on down. My boots, puttees, drawers were all frozen so hard I could not get them on, but luckily I had some Gilgit boots.

The valley now became much flatter and as we got lower the

snow became less and less. It was snowing when we started, but the sun gradually forced its way through the clouds and the afternoon became quite fine. We got well down into the Kustai valley and went on till the snow had nearly disappeared before we pitched camp among the fir trees. We then lit huge fires to dry all our wet clothes and get something to eat. John had a slight attack of mountain sickness at about 13,000 feet but it did not last long. I shall certainly never trust the word of a Kazak again as to distance or excellence of a road.

Friday, October 3rd
We did not make an early start as the march today was not to be a long one, only to Tola Bai's house on the Kustai plateau. We went down the Kustai valley for about five miles through magnificent fir woods, the trees here growing to an immense height. The chief difficulty in getting through these fir woods consists in the fallen giants which everywhere are littered about forming almost impenetrable abatis. The going today was very slippery thanks to the half-frozen slush and snow in the woods. We then left the Kustai valley and climbed high up on to the Kustai plateau, passing through more woods. Here John spotted a blackcock close to the path, which I proceeded to gather in for the larder, as I am getting rather tired of stag's meat, which though quite tender is very tasteless.

We pitched our camp in an open space amid the fir woods and on a little spur and from my tent I command the most beautiful views over plain and dark fir woods and snowy peaks. Sunset this evening was very beautiful but cold. The day was again quite cloudless. On the way we passed a number of auls: on arrival at the first, Tola Bai set up the most awful howling in which all the inmates joined. The womenfolk covered themselves with a white cloth and continued singing and howling all the time that I was there. I found out afterwards that the headman had died about three weeks ago and they keep up the mourning for a month and all strangers that pass by join in. We are quite close to Tola Bai's house.

Saturday, October 4th

A day of rest. The sun came very early to this camp and woke me up. The day was a deliciously warm one, quite cloudless and in spite of the snow still lying in patches, I was only too glad to sit in the shade. This is really a most delightful climate, these cold, frosty nights and gloriously clear warm days. It is good to be alive and I should like to linger on here, lazing away for some time, but I am afraid I must wander slowly back to the grey skies of England.

During the morning I paid personally for the Kazak horses that I hired, exacting receipts, so that these Kazaks should not say that I had gone away without paying. On counting up the damage suffered in crossing the Karasir pass, I find one bearskin torn and the claws missing, three roe deer masks, two sheep and one ibex all lost when the pony fell. The horns, however, that had been sent here a month ago are all safe. Tola Bai yesterday presented me with a sheep, which the camp enjoyed. While Tola Bai was away with me, some Kazaks came and looted his camp, beating his son and wife and carrying off his daughter. I have taken a full account of the whole matter with the names of the culprits and am going to make a fuss at Kuldja about it. The Kazaks are jealous because English people always take Tola Bai who is by far the best Kazak hunter.

A furious gale has set in while I am writing this after dinner, upsetting the lamp and inkpot and covering me with ink.

Sunday, October 5th

The Kazaks had nearly all moved lower down to their winter quarters in the valleys and the uplands were deserted. Wild pig had been everywhere rooting in the grass, apparently digging up the field mice which abound. Hawks, falcons and eagles are very common now in this month and September. The hunters catch them in large numbers by means of snares set round a pigeon or partridge. The Kazaks are very fond of hawking and big prices are given for a good bird. Tola Bai's son produced a fine eagle which they have trained to catch foxes and roe-deer.

Monday, October 6th

To my surprise in spite of being so low down, there was a very heavy white frost at night: but as soon as the sun came out it became quite warm and we had a beautiful day. I started off early by myself to look for partridges, when I came across some pheasants: on my firing at them, they flew down into some long grass. Two Kazaks heard the shot and, seeing the pheasants come down, promptly rode up and marked the spot, so that when I got them I had two easy right and lefts, to their great delight when they saw all four birds fall.

They asked me if I would like any partridge and on my replying yes, took me to some bushes under a cliff where I managed to secure two chukar and a hen pheasant. The pheasant fell out in the Kok-su and one Kazak boldly plunged in and rescued it. He invited me to his aul where I was given junket to drink and tea flavoured with milk and salt, which was first well boiled: it was the nastiest decoction that I have drunk for some time.

Out of the five pheasants four were cocks: they were much whiter than the English pheasant, with many white feathers in the wing. We then rode for some hours over the downs towards the Tekes, putting up two quail en route, both of which I missed.

Passing the mandarin's house, I found that he had come back from Kuldja and also that there were a number of Kazaks there, who were frightened that I was going to make a fuss over Tola Bai. I, therefore, called on the mandarin who was very friendly and gave me tea and koumiss. I told him the whole facts of the case, which he had not heard before, and said that I would take the matter up to Kuldja which seemed to upset him. He said that he hated these Kazaks: they stole, they murdered and they lied and were always giving trouble. On leaving him he gave me a present of potatoes and onions and sent a sheep to camp: I gave him four of the pheasants I had shot in the morning.

On the way to camp I shot a couple of partridges and a hare to keep the larder well supplied. The mandarin had promised to come and pay me a visit and he came in time for dinner. As we had only just pitched camp, the menu was not an elaborate one: sardines – pea soup – roast blackcock (which was excellent and very tender) with potatoes and carrots, preserved greengages and to drink I had nothing but brandy which he rather enjoyed.

Tuesday, October 7th

I got up early to go after pheasants which I was told were here in great numbers. In the evening they were mostly in the millet fields which had been cut: here they were very wild and kept getting up 50 to 100 yards ahead. They were, if possible, worse runners than the English ones and I could see the brutes in sixes and sevens running along a hundred yards ahead.

The people around here are all Kalmucks: we seem to have left the Kazaks behind. The Kalmucks are only too anxious to show one the pheasants as I fancy they do their crops a considerable amount of harm.

Wednesday, October 8th

Today I had more luck, for several Kalmucks came to help, who thoroughly enjoyed the show, but they always went first for the empty cartridge cases, before they thought of going for the birds. In a couple of hours I got eighteen birds, ten cocks and eight hens. Most of the cocks too were old birds which pleased me, as I am always fond of outwitting an old cock pheasant. Instead of thirty-three birds, I ought to have got at least fifty if I had been shooting well and with several guns one would get a very fine bag.

These will be very useful for presents in Kuldja and for the customs officer. The bear is getting extremely fat and good tempered with all the food that he is getting now: he is an object of great interest to everyone. The magpies which abound everywhere always come and have a look at him and chatter round him to his disgust, but of course he never succeeds in catching them.

Thursday, October 9th

A frosty night followed by a late start in the morning. Before we left a Kalmuck came up with a gourd of arrack: he said he had no sheep but brought this spirit for me: I just tasted it and found it incredibly nasty. It was made from sour milk which had been distilled and is a drink which the Kalmucks like very much and on which they can get very drunk.

Our path led first across the irrigated plain, on which millets and barley are chiefly grown. I saw a little tobacco also which they use as snuff and eat and also enough opium for home consumption.

A little after three we pitched camp in the bottom of the valley close to the road. I gave John some castor oil, as he had been complaining of stomach ache and on asking what he had been eating, was told the insides of the pheasants, so I was not surprised, as I had found inside one an undigested snake between 8 and 10 inches long.

Friday, October 10th

A dull grey morning and a slight drizzle but we got off early before 8 a.m. The path led on down through a narrow rocky gorge: there were berberis and spiraea bushes on either side but no trees. They use the spiraea bush a great deal in these parts for the making of whip handles.

We passed a number of small mills owned by Sarts and then came out onto the bare slopes that gradually descend to the Ili river. The day remained luckily cloudy, as otherwise it might have been very hot down here. The pack ponies came along well as the going was easy.

Most of the people that I passed mistook me for an Afghan, as I was wearing a puggaree, much to the amusement of my following. In the afternoon we came to the Ili river and this time we were lucky in finding a ferry boat ready and on the right side. We crossed the river some miles higher up than we did the last time, just below the junction of the Kash river. It did not take us long to unload everything and put it in the boat: the horses swam over first and then we crossed.

The river here is now only a little over 100 yards wide, but swift and deep and of a bluey-green colour, very different in size and colour to what it was in June. We camped a few hundred yards away after landing.

Next day they reached Kuldja once more and Howard-Bury stayed at the Mission House with Father Raemdonck.

Sunday, October 12th

As a barber could not be found, Father Raemdonck volunteered to cut my hair and beard for me, both of which were very long. Before I knew where I was, I found my head almost clean shorn. The beard was a matter of considerable difficulty and took a long time to get off. While having breakfast my caravan man came to tell me that five of my horses had been stolen during the night, together with seventeen others belonging to other people. Now we come back to so-called civilisation, everything gets stolen: the night before we had a sheep stolen.

I wrote at once to the Russian Consul and to the Shengwan and they have sent seven men to try and catch the thieves. The thieves were apparently five in number and came armed with rifles and drove the ponies away. The man that was watching them was too afraid to do anything. All the highest Chinese officials here belong to a society called the Kolahui which consists chiefly of thieves, so probably very little may be done, though possibly they may think that an Englishman passing through may cause a lot of trouble and so they may bestir themselves.

I sent the Russian Consul and the Shengwan both presents of pheasants, as I have such a lot of them. In the evening eight of the ponies were found locked up in an enclosure near here, three of which were mine. In the evening I dined alone with the Consul, who is most kind and hospitable. He tells me that the authority of Peking here is still very shadowy and that in the government of the province there is quite anarchy. There is plenty of opium grown around here and also near Prejvalsk of which a great deal is smuggled across the frontier, but he thinks the Russians are going to stop it in Russian territory, not for the moral welfare of the Chinese but because he is afraid that Russian subjects may learn the habit. I had a fine moonlight walk back through Kuldja: I never saw anywhere so many dogs as there were in the streets, but I had a good stick with me.

Monday, October 13th
Spent the morning trying to arrange the horns in the smallest possible space for a box, which I am getting a Chinese carpenter to make for me. I then went to the Russo-Asiatic Bank where it took me an hour to get some money on my letter of credit. Tea and conversation on every other subject are indispensable, before the serious work of cashing a cheque begins. At the post office I found two boxes of most welcome chocolates from Johnny and Charles, but I had to pay Russian duty on them though this is China. I had lunch with the Russian Consul and did not get away till late. Sixteen out of the twenty-two ponies have been found.

Tuesday, October 14th
Spent the morning in writing letters. The weather here still is delicious, warm, sunny days but cool nights, though it does not quite freeze yet. In the afternoon I took a walk round the town and through the bazaars, but saw very little of interest in the shops or streets. Water melons are one of the commonest articles and they must grow them in enormous numbers. Skins and leather too are another great article of trade, but I saw no good furs, only sheep and goat skins with a few foxes and an occasional bear skin. In the evening I went to supper with the Consul, where besides him and his wife were three Cossack officers belonging to the Cossack guard and detachment here. We had quite a cheery evening, for they had a very good gramophone, which played many Russian dances.

Wednesday, October 15th
Another lovely day. Went out to see how the boxes for the horns were getting on and found that they are making them of wood between 2 and 3 inches thick: the box alone will weigh a ton nearly. Spent most of the day writing letters. I intend if possible to start tomorrow for Tsarnakai, but am very doubtful about getting there.

Thursday, October 16th
A grey day with heavy clouds and a cold wind blowing. I am afraid that it is snowing on all the mountains around, as at times a drizzle is falling. The ponies did not arrive till very late so that we could

not get off before 11.30 a.m. I have only three pony loads, as I am travelling lightly and do not expect to be away for more than a fortnight.

Before I left, a man arrived from the Shengwan with his card and presents of tea and Russian biscuits. The remaining ponies have not yet turned up though I am sure the Shengwan's men know where they are and who stole them. The little bear is being left behind this time under Father Raemdonck's charge.

About three miles from Kuldja we crossed the Ili by a ferry at a place where it was only 70 yards wide. There were two backwaters there which made the crossing easy. Soon after we passed through a large walled village called Koir Sumun, inhabited by people from Manchuria and remarkably clean. Just as it was getting dark we reached the big village of Kainak inhabited by Taranchis or Sarts. Seeing a nice garden, I asked the owner if I might camp there. He, of course, gave me permission and soon sent out some water melons and a large bowl of most delicious soup with meat and macaroni in it.

This village and that of Djalgustai have a great reputation for hospitality in these parts. Near the Ili there were some fields growing a giant millet of a reddish-brown colour.

Friday, October 17th
A lovely hot autumn day. During the night a dog came and carried off four pheasants, three partridges and a lot of fat. The whole was inside John's tent and there were three men sleeping there, but these people sleep so soundly that if a cannon went off in their tent, they would not hear it.

We did not start till 9 a.m. as I went to pay a visit to the owner of the garden. These Taranchi houses are roomy and very clean inside. The walls are of mud and the roof is supported by beams and cross pieces, on the top of which are reeds. Inside, half of the floor of the living room is raised and in a corner is a shallow iron pan under which when a fire is lighted, water is very quickly raised to boiling point. The hot air goes under the raised floor and on this floor the family sleep.

After going for about 9 miles we came to Djalgustai and I went with Tola Bai to raise a hunter. Not finding him at home, I left Tola Bai to wait and went on with John to where another hunter lived. We found him at home and he said he would come with us, if we would come in and drink some tea. While the tea was being made ready, nearly half the village came in to have a look: the tea was made with salt and sour milk and extremely nasty, so that I did not drink much.

On this short and somewhat abortive hunting trip the Colonel "saw a very fine specimen of an ermine with a mouse in his mouth, but he eluded me". Tola Bai told him the Chonochai valley "was quite deserted being close to the Russian frontier, as the people were afraid of thieves, and was in consequence full of game. But to my disgust I saw human tracks everywhere and then half a dozen Kalmuck auls . . . So much for believing what Tola Bai says."

And it was not just Kalmucks. The Chinese had posted frontier guards to catch the horse thieves, but "now that the snow has come down and the passes over the Russian side are closed, they spend their time in hunting, as they have Government rifles and nothing else to do."

Thursday, October 23rd
Today I started back towards Kuldja as I find it no use going after stag here. Just before I left camp, the captain of the Kalmuck guard came to see me and to express his regrets that he was away when I arrived. He has sixty men under him to patrol this section of the frontier.

Our path today led us along the bottom of the Chonochai valley which is very narrow and winding with precipitous sides which forced us to cross the river innumerable times. After going about 11 miles we came to a fair sized village called Mazar, where there is also a small fort. Here we left the valley and turned off to the east crossing a high plateau which slopes gradually down towards the Ili. On the way I shot a hare, a pigeon and two chukar.

On looking at my expenditure, I find that the cost of feeding myself, John and two other servants is just a shilling a day or an average of 3d a head. I am not using up any stores either except jam, so that living in this country is pretty cheap.

On arriving at a small valley called Kichik Buri where were water and trees, I camped. Shortly after a Kazak comes up and wants to know why I have come there to his winter ground. We tied his horse up and kept him in camp till after dark, when he humbly apologised for his rudeness and promised to show us the road tomorrow. I had only threatened to take him with me to the Has-a-chu (the head of the Kazaks) at Kurai, but this effectually terrified him and made him eat humble pie. The day was fine but the wind was cold and it clouded over in the afternoon.

Friday, October 24th
A very heavy white frost during the night: the day was a hazy one for this country and a cold wind blew across the plains. Soon after starting we passed through the village of Kichik Buri, which is now in ruins, but before the Tungan rising, it was quite a flourishing place. Here I managed to shoot three sand grouse: throughout the day we kept seeing numbers of them but elsewhere they were too wary to allow one to get within shot, as they fed in the stubble fields.

We left all paths and took a line across country, there being no obstacle to the pack ponies except the countless little irrigation channels which intersect the country in every direction. At one time this must have been a very prosperous country and it only needs population now to become so again.

The Kazak who was so rude last night came again this morning before I left with many more apologies for his rudeness. In the afternoon I shot a couple of brown partridges and later on I saw a great bustard, but before I could get my rifle he flew away. Just as it was getting dark we arrived at Sibi village where we found wood and water.

Saturday, October 25th
A bitter wind was blowing in the morning and a dull grey sky foretold a change in the weather. Hurriedly packing up and starting we passed close to the first village of the Sipos: they are a flourishing community and have a number of villages near here, all regular walled towns. They speak a language of their own and came

many years ago from Mongolia: they are supposed also to have Persian blood in them from the old Persian conquerors who married Chinese wives. Near here I saw two more of the greater bustard, but they would not allow me within 200 yards of them. Passing another walled Sipo village I shot a cock pheasant in the crops. The tall reddish brown millet is still standing everywhere and is often not cut till after the snow has fallen. The soil here is a rich loess and bears very good crops but after it has had water on it, is impossible to ride over.

I saw numbers of duck in the rice fields, but they had too sharp eyes to allow me to get near enough for a shot. We crossed the Ili by the same ferry as the last time, carrying eight ponies, twenty people, two carts and their loads and all my pony loads. The boat was loaded to within a couple of inches of the water, but we crossed without accident. I then trotted on ahead into Kuldja, just in time to get lunch from Father Raemdonck. The rain started in soon after dark, so that we have just got to a roof in time.

Sunday, October 26th
A most beautiful day after the night's rain and the mountains are wonderfully clear and sprinkled with fresh snow. The mud in the streets is awful, inches deep.

We were discussing this morning the iniquities of the self-appointed local government. The rulers as far as governing the district is concerned are quite hopeless: all they do is to get rich as fast as they can by issuing paper money, which they change into Russian silver. The seer and the rouble used to be about the same value: when I arrived four months ago the rouble was worth 2½ seers: the other day it was worth 4 seers and now it fluctuates between 3½ and 4 seers. Besides this they are all thieves and accept presents from all the other thieves in order not to be punished.

At lunch time the Aksakal came in with the information that there has been another revolution in Kurai, 20 miles from here and the seat of the government of the province and that several of the generals and self-appointed governors including Fungtaming had been killed. Of course there is great excitement over this, but I do not imagine that much more will happen, as the authors of this counter revolution are probably acting under orders from Peking and it will be an excellent thing for the country if the present rulers have been killed. At the news, the price of the seer at once rose, in the hopes that the Chinese Government will guarantee the paper money.

I went out into the bazaar with Father Raemdonck to buy a couple of larks to take back with me. The larks of these parts are very large and beautiful songsters, much finer than our European ones: they imitate too every animal's cry and birds' songs.

Monday, October 27th

There is not much fresh news about the revolution in Kurai; Fungtaming, Li Chang and his brother and a number of soldiers have been killed, but otherwise all is quiet. Business goes on here as usual, though a number of the people are very frightened that the bad characters may make mischief while affairs are thus unsettled.

The present counter revolution has rather upset Russian prospects of getting further concessions in this district, for from the late rulers in return for a loan of two million roubles at 6 per cent, they were to get concessions for all the minerals in Ili, which are very considerable. There are five coal mines that are being worked within a radius of 12 miles of Kuldja, but in the most primitive fashion, there are mountains of copper near by; silver and gold is also found in considerable quantities and many other valuable minerals.

Tuesday, October 28th

Another lovely day. Bought a lark in the morning and a telega in the afternoon for 50 roubles on which to put my horns. We finished packing up the horns which are in an immense box, of which the weight is unknown. Very little further news about the revolution, except that Madoling the author of it who is a Taranchi has caused the heads of the decapitated former rulers to be exposed on posts in the city. The people generally dislike the Tungans who are thus brought into power. The Tungans in 1870 massacred the whole population of Ili and people do not like or trust them now. They have already forbidden the sale of pork in the city.

Thursday, October 30th

A dull grey day. I had meant to start this morning but the bear's box was not finished. Father Raemdonck worked hard at it, as the Sart carpenter was not doing it properly, but by mid-day it was finished. We then had a long and difficult job in getting the box of horns on to the cart. It is very heavy and I am much afraid of an accident en route, as the roads are awful. I went and had lunch with the consul, who was most agreeable. The Chang Chung had received direct orders from Peking to kill these revolutionaries, but he was too kind (or afraid) and showed them the order and begged them to fly over the frontier. They refused thinking themselves safe and that nobody would dare touch them, but the news leaked out and Madoling with his soldiers came early in the morning and killed them and about twenty other mandarins. Everyone was made to speak before they were killed: those that spoke with a northern accent were spared, but those that spoke with the southern tongue were slain.

Friday, October 31st

Everything was loaded up by 8 a.m., the big telega and my tarantass were quite full up and we started off gaily, I ahead in the tarantass. I had got as far as the post office when Father Raemdonck comes galloping up on his pony to say that the telega is smashed up not a hundred yards after starting. Like all Russians, the drivers love to start off at full gallop, but unfortunately the road here was narrow and there were two heavy Chinese carts in the way. My cart went straight against the solid Chinese cart smashing the axle and part of the side. The Starosta who had supplied the horses then turned nasty and said that he would do nothing, as it was not his fault. I went off to the Consul at once and told him about the accident. He at once sent for the Starosta, told him that he was to make me a new axle and to give me horses when it was finished. Everything was then taken back to the Mission House and a Russian carpenter came and spent the day in making a new axle.

While we were at lunch, Mungtagen, a mandarin over the Mongols, came and paid the Father a visit with the Japanese and shortly after when we were watching the work on the telega, Fungtagen the new Taotai with an escort of soldiers and a mounted follower carrying a huge leather case fully 18 inches long, in which were the Taotai's visiting cards, drove up. They are both good men, who now will put down the lawlessness and thieving that is rampant in the district. Today there was the sound of cannon at Kurai, so there must be more fighting going on there.

Saturday, November 1st
We actually did manage to get off this morning, Father Raemdonck rode a few miles along with us to see that everything was all right. The morning was fine and the views towards the mountains freshly covered with snow were very striking. Though the weather has been fine with us, it has been unsettled in the mountains and long strips of clouds soon formed half way up the mountains, below, everything was a deep blue and above quite white.

The road was in a shocking state and we took six hours to do the 50 versts, the dust being everywhere many inches deep. There is a great deal of traffic on this road and we met numerous carts loaded with coal, and the equivalent of motor bus companies ply along the road with wooden carts covered over with matting and drawn by three horses. At the half way halting place we met two Cossacks who were evidently hard up for money, as one of them sold his shirt for 49 kopecks, which my driver bought, and the other sold a pair of gloves.

The trees here are still very green as the season is a late one and the snow on the mountains is not below 7,000 feet. We passed through Kurai, which showed but few outward signs of Revolution beyond that there were soldiers and policemen everywhere. Now everyone goes about with a rifle and it is the exception to meet a horseman unarmed. The rifle is either slung or carried under the leg with the muzzle to the ground.

On arrival at Suidum we found no horses and so perforce have to wait till tomorrow. Our troubles are only just beginning and I am afraid the journey to Tashkent will last a long time. In the afternoon I took a walk through Suidum, a walled town but with few signs of prosperity within the walls. It is smaller than Kuldja and everybody seems engaged in gambling or playing cards. I bought a pack.

Sunday, November 2nd

We started off before dawn and had not done 20 yards before the wooden pole under the telega split and though we tried to tie it up with rope, were not successful, with the result that the front and back wheels kept going off at different angles. In spite of only going at a walk, the cart twice overturned and we took ten hours to get to Khorgos. On the way we passed strings of camels going towards Kuldja, for quite two hours. There must have been between 2,000 and 3,000 of them. They were in the charge of Mongols from the north and were fine looking beasts, some almost black, others nearly white and with long shaggy hair.

The bear caused great excitement wherever we went and crowds assembled to look at him whenever we stopped. At the Chinese frontier our passport was examined and then we had the broad and stony bed of the Khorgos river to cross to the Russian side. The morning had been fine and sunny, but now a violent gale arose, which blew straight in our faces and a cold sleet fell which soon turned to snow.

At the Russian frontier after a short delay, in which our papers were examined, all our cases and goods were passed without examination. Finding the post station full of travellers, we went to another house kept by Government for Government servants and here after some demur we were admitted. The cart was unloaded and turned over in order to repair it, but the repairs were not finished before dark. If we go on at this rate, it will take us over a month to get to Tashkent. Being Sunday, I met a number of Russian moujiks very much the worse for liquor, who could hardly stand.

Monday, November 3rd

Most of the morning was spent in repairing the broken cart as the damages were more extensive than we had imagined. The night had been a very cold one and the ground was white with snow in the morning. This seemed to vanish during the day as it did not melt, but was apparently absorbed into the dry air.

Everybody so objected to the big box of horns and it certainly did make the cart top heavy, that I took out all the horns here and tied them firmly up on the cart and left the box behind. Since then, no one has objected to the weight, as they do not look heavy like this. At one o'clock we were ready to start: I was looking after the bear at the time, when the horses of my tarantass started off, the driver who was on the box was unable to stop them, they got out of the courtyard safely, turned sharp right and went at full gallop down the street; the driver then either fell off or threw himself off and the carriage lurched into some young poplar trees breaking them down: it luckily missed the big trees. The whole village, meanwhile, turned out and gave good chase. The horses crossed two small bridges safely, passed the customs house and then luckily turned up a small street which ended in a garden and there they stopped.

The damage done to the carriage was very little and we were able to start off soon after. The wind was bitter and it snowed at times. We did the two stages to Jarkent, arriving there just as it was getting dark. I sent John off to find the head of the police to show him our passports, but he could not find him, so I sent him off again after dinner and he ran him to ground in a liquor shop, trying to catch drunkards. He at once came to the post house and gave us leave to proceed.

Tuesday, November 4th

A very hard frost during the night and all the streams were frozen over. We passed a squadron of Cossacks with coloured flags on lances, a few carrying rifles and swords. They were followed by a travelling soup kitchen. I could not make out what they were going to do, but on enquiry found that they were going to beat for wild pig in the woods and high grass which extend for some miles around Jarkent. We managed to cover four stages today, as they changed horses more quickly than usual, and we actually got some cutlets, for lunch. The country in parts much resembled part of the Punjab and at one time we might really have been going through the Khyber pass. Most of the way we gradually ascended and at times we passed patches of fresh snow: towards evening it froze hard and we did the last stage by moonlight getting in at nine o'clock.

Wednesday, November 5th

We started off very early in the morning, hoping to do a good day's journey, but forgot that we were on these cursed Russian roads where Postmasters do everything they can to stop and hinder an Englishman, giving preference to every Russian that comes along. The first stage was over the plain and the sunrise was very beautiful, first the snowy peaks turned a pale pink, then a deeper colour and finally white. We covered the first stage quickly and then got a change of horses. The next stage was over a pass and as we approached we got into snow. The wind must have blown strongly from the north for there were very deep drifts in every sheltered spot on the south. The climb up the pass was very steep; here we met some time expired soldiers returning to Siberia and also a heavy post. We exchanged horses and came rapidly down the north side of the pass. Here the snow was lying deeper and they were using sleighs.

On arrival at the post house of Altunmeli, we were told that there were no horses, but that we could have some at five o'clock. So we spent the afternoon in covering up the horns with cloth and in repacking them, for they were getting badly rubbed. At five o'clock, we asked if the horses were ready, but were told that we could not have any till the following morning. Some other travellers arrived and were given horses: they were not Government officials. When an engineer arrived, he was given horses at once, but the Postmaster delights in making English people wait. These Russian post-roads were certainly the invention of the devil in order to make one lose one's temper, but being unable to speak the language it is quite useless to do so.

Thursday, November 6th

A strong north-east wind blew all night which brought up the grey clouds and it looked as though it was going to snow. Instead, however, it turned very mild and the roads became a slush of water and snow. The wheelwright arrived back during the night and I was able to get the rims of the wheels, which were very loose, tightened up. This prevented our starting till ten o'clock. We managed to cover two stages, the going was very heavy: the country was gently undulating and excellent pasture land. Enormous herds of horses were grazing on the grass that stood out of the snow. After going about 40 versts we came to the watershed at about 4,600 feet and had a wide view over the enormous Ili valley. We then gradually descended to the stage at Karachekinskaia, where we were told that there were no horses. Eight other travellers that arrived afterwards were given horses and drivers. Thus is the English traveller treated when travelling in Russia!

Friday, November 7th

A beautiful morning and with a hard frost which made the going easy at first, as the snow was frozen. The road was much better and smoother than usual and we got along well. The snow gradually disappeared as we got low down and when we reached Iliski, there was practically none. We crossed the Ili by a fine wooden bridge and reached the big village of Iliski. Here the Postmaster objected to the bear, as he said it would frighten the horses. His objections were, however, overruled and we covered a third stage. Here we spent the night.

Saturday, November 8th

The bear causes the most extraordinary excitement wherever we go: the whole population, when we stop, come to see it and all the roads are blocked for other traffic. Starting early in the morning, we slowly covered the remaining stage to Verny. There had been a hard white frost in the night and the sunrise was very pretty with the lofty range of snow covered mountains in front of us. The situation of Verny at the foot of these mountains and surrounded with trees is very picturesque. But alas, as we approached Verny, the roads became worse and worse. The mud got deeper and deeper and the holes larger, till finally we stuck in the main street of the town. The place has the makings of a very fine town: it is well laid out and there are plenty of trees along the roads. The houses are, however, miserable for the most part, though here and there a house or a church stands out in great contrast, with clean white walls and green roofs. The streets and the roads are, however, beyond description and how the Russians can exist with roads like this is more than I can understand.

We got horses soon and came on another stage over an execrable road: they are starting to put down great rounded river boulders which makes the going still worse. The plain round Verny is extremely fertile and is celebrated for its apples. The second stage beyond Verny we wanted to make a short cut across the mountains to Tokmak and so we went to the Zimstvo. The owner from whom we should have had to hire horses wanted too much so we came on the ordinary post road. Here we heard that warnings had been issued all along the road to everyone that an English gentleman and an Indian were coming along, and that no information is to be given them. The result is that if we ask, if there is any shooting or the distance of a place, the reply always is "I don't know".

Sunday, November 9th
We did a short stage of 19½ versts in the early hours of the morning and then had to wait for three hours before going on. The Postmaster at the next station then objected to the bear and much talk and silver lining was needed.

Monday, November 10th
After a night of rain, the morning broke with heavy clouds and a Scotch mist; we took most of the day in covering two fairly short stages to Pispek, for the state of the roads was awful and we had to go at a walk most of the time. Never have I seen such mud in any other country and the larger the town, the worse the mud.

Tuesday, November 11th
A glorious morning after all the rain with a slight white frost. The road was everywhere in the most filthy condition and we kept skidding and side-slipping badly in the mud. We kept all day to the

north of a fine range of snow-covered mountains on which live plenty of ibex. For 90 versts we kept along what was almost a continuous village. Most of it had sprung up within the last two or three years and consisted of settlers brought by the Russian government and put down here. They seemed to be all doing well and had built themselves nice thatched cottages. The country is everywhere very fertile, with plenty of water and a good rainfall. The place was full of children, strong and healthy, and I should think that this country has a great future before it when the railway comes here. Next year they say that they hope to have construction trains running as far as Pispek and passenger trains in two or three years' time, but I doubt it as I have seen no signs of work. The bear causes the greatest interest all along the road and at one time we had an escort of quite 200 Kirghiz boys galloping along beside the cart. This road is much prettier than the Semipalatinsk road is, there are trees everywhere and fine snowy mountains.

Wednesday, November 12th

We had some difficulty in hiring horses here and when we did get them, they were miserable specimens and we took all day in getting to Merke, a distance of 26 versts. On the way we saw a curious Kirghiz custom; when a person of importance dies or is married, a goat is killed, which is then carried off on horseback and all the guests ride after the goat to try and pull it to pieces, the result is something like a football scrimmage on horseback – often at full gallop, tearing in every direction across the country, it is quite a common thing for people to get killed at this game.*

The mud on the roads was bad, often a foot deep, and the carriage kept skidding. They tell me that the roads are not nearly as bad as in spring, when the mud is 2 feet deep and it is often impossible to cover 12 versts, going all day.

On arrival at Merke, we spent a long time bargaining for horses: some Russian travellers were very good in helping us and we

---

* What Howard-Bury describes here is a game of *buzkashi*, still played today by Kirghiz and their neighbours on the Russian borders of Tajikistan and the remoter Chinese reaches of Sinkiang Province.

eventually managed to hire horses to the railway station at Kabul Sai, 400 versts, for the two carriages for 110 roubles. As the people from whom we hired the horses had a cart of their own, we transferred all the horns to their cart and sold ours for 20 roubles. One of the travellers gave me some butter, which was the first that I had tasted since the beginning of June. I had no idea butter could be so good. I had a very disturbed night as travellers kept arriving and all the rooms were packed with people sleeping on the floor or anywhere.

Thursday, November 13th
The country was flat and averaging about 2,500 feet in height. We started off early but only managed to cover 35 versts as we kept the same horses all the time. I had to take my meals whenever I could, at serais or in Sart tea shops and very nasty they were. Everyone that one talks with, seems full of revolutionary ideas and their only wish seems to be to get rid of their rulers as quickly as possible, whether they be officers or Government officials. I took tea in the evening in the house of a moujik: the interior was very clean but hot and the walls decorated with sacred pictures. We started off again at midnight.

Friday, November 14th
We travelled along slowly all night: the road in places was very bad: at dawn we stopped for two or three hours for breakfast. Here the civil engineers that I have met several times on the road insisted on my having breakfast with them and they produced every kind of wine and liqueur, which I was made to taste.

Saturday, November 15th
At ten o'clock we stopped for three hours at a Russian farm house to feed the horses and have something to eat. I am getting nearly starved as I had only a sardine for dinner yesterday but managed to get two eggs for breakfast which have to last me all day. We started again at one o'clock and took seven and a half hours to cover the remaining stage into Auliata. The going was dreadful. Auliata appears to be quite a large place with fine avenues of trees. We stopped at a new hotel that is just being built and is not yet

147

finished. I was given quite a clean room but had the greatest difficulty in getting anything to eat.

Sunday, November 16th

One of our horses is ill and the owners went out and tried to buy another one to replace it, but could not succeed in doing so. We are, therefore unable to get on and have to hire another lot of horses. This we only succeeded in doing with great difficulty and by paying an exorbitant price, as the roads now are almost impassable. We eventually got a man to take us with seven horses to Kabul Sai, buying our tarantass there for 80 roubles and we pay him 30 roubles more.

I went out in the afternoon to lay in a stock of provisions for the journey in case we are snowed up. The town is a pretty one and full of fine avenues of trees, but several of the roads were blocked by trees that had fallen across them, broken down by the weight of snow. There is a very big Sart bazaar here, with the streets covered over with matting, but the huge heaps of snow underneath that had been shovelled off the roofs made progression difficult. I bought several specimens of the Tashkent wines to sample them and I find some of them not at all bad.

Monday, November 17th

About an inch of snow fell during the night, but the morning was fine. Everything looked so pretty all covered with snow in the bright sunshine, but the state of the roads with 8 to 10 inches of fresh snow was awful. We left the post-road and took a short cut which for the first stage was very bad and stony, across wide river beds. Just as we were starting on the second stage, my tarantass overturned breaking the shaft: this caused further delay. The larks who were inside were, I am glad to say, unhurt.

Tuesday, November 18th

The first part of the night I slept well, but it turned very cold after midnight and everything was frozen solid, so at three o'clock I awoke the others who were snoring loudly inside and said that we would start. At first there was a thick fog, but as we rose this disappeared. We climbed up a narrow valley rising about 1,000 feet on to a broad plateau. Here it was very cold and the hoar frost had covered everything with large crystals.

After 18 versts we reached a Russian village where I was very glad to get a samovar and some hot tea. The next stage was a long one and after crossing a wide plain we slowly climbed up to 4,000 feet, when we crossed the Chacha pass. This pass is much dreaded at this time of year as it is subject to violent storms and on arrival at the top we found a bitter gale blowing: this continued all night, but luckily came from behind us.

We reached the village of Chapnak soon after dark. There was luckily an inn close to the serai and I went there for the few hours that we remained. The beds in this part of the world are not comfortable, usually consisting of planks of wood stretched across a framework and occasionally in very superior places, of wire netting.

Wednesday, November 19th
We left again at 3 a.m. in a gale. It was freezing hard, but it was a dry cold and less felt than yesterday's. This side of the pass there is less snow and as a consequence the large frozen ruts were dreadful and I was black and blue from bruises by the morning.

Friday, November 21st
We started off at three in the morning and with only one halt in the middle of the day managed to cover the 64 versts to Kabul Sai, where we struck the railway. The country was uninteresting, very undulating and without the sign of a tree anywhere. We gradually left the snow behind and at Kabul Sai there was none. We only arrived there after dark and had some trouble in carrying over everything to the station. The face of the Stationmaster and his staff when he saw our miscellaneous luggage was very comical, for the horns were all loose and covered the station platform and this together with a small bear was quite too much for him. However, after a while he became quite genial and allowed the bear to travel as passenger's luggage. We had to wait till two in the morning before the train came and then it was a great rush getting everything in in five minutes, for the station is only a small one, as the junction

for the new line to Verny and Semipalatinsk is 20 versts away. The train was so heated that it has since given me a bad cold.

Saturday, November 22nd
We arrived at Tashkent at dawn and after collecting all the luggage drove to the town which is some way from the station. I went to the Hotel Russia which is a new one and remarkably clean. The town Tashkent is a large one with about 260,000 inhabitants: the streets are broad and well laid out with plenty of trees and open spaces: most of the roads too are metalled which is a blessing. The town gives one rather an idea of a cantonment as the houses are mostly one-storied, though well-built and they are surrounded by trees and in their own grounds.

I went to see the Diplomatic Officer (M. Semionoff), to see if I would be allowed to proceed to Samarkand and Bokhara. He did not speak either French or German and only a very little English, so that conversation was only carried on with difficulty, but he gave me another permit to show to the police and also looked up a file which they had about me with instructions from St. Petersburg, so that all my movements are well known.

I then arranged for boxes to be made to carry the horns and skins to London: the carpenter promised to have these ready by Monday. In the afternoon I drove out to the old Sart town: it lies some miles away, but the road there is through narrow and winding streets all the way, often so narrow that two carts cannot pass. Everywhere are numbers of curious high-wheeled carts, the wheels being about eight feet in diameter: in the shafts is one small pony on which the driver sits with his feet on the shafts and his knees tucked up under his chin, giving him a comical appearance, as the wheels of the cart are higher than his head. In the Sart town the streets are all roofed over, making it very dark underneath. As they run up and down hill, the effect is very picturesque. Every available inch of space is taken up by shops of all kinds.

Sunday, November 23rd
A very wet day, so I did not get up till late. A Russian cotton planter, who is staying in the Hotel and who speaks good English, asked to

see me, as he is anxious to visit India. He wants very much to carry me off to Kokand in Ferghana where he has his plantation and to show me some of the well-developed parts of these provinces.

In the morning we went to the museum here which is only a small one, but it has an interesting collection of old weapons, coins and antiquities from these parts: there were also collections of birds and animals, but only a few of them were well set up. There was a fine specimen of the long haired tiger from the Amu-daria, but my sheep, ibex, wapiti and roe-deer were better than any in the museum. There were good specimens of the greater bustard, snowcock, pelicans and flamingoes.

In the evening I went with a couple of civil engineers to a cinematograph show close by: it is run by a Grand Duke who is in exile here and who has been here now for over thirty years. From the queer stories that have been told me about him, he is a very eccentric personage. The best features in the show were some peasant songs, sung by really good singers.

Irrigation seems to be the most important topic of these parts and very large systems have already been brought to completion, as without water very little will grow. Engineers are now everywhere arranging for fresh irrigation systems from the Amu-daria, which has an inexhaustible supply of water. Ferghana which is the richest province has already a very good system and the cotton grown there is extremely good: it is the Egyptian kind and better, they say, than it is in Egypt. There are only two Englishmen resident in Turkestan: one is a teacher here and the other is in the cotton business at Kokand.

Monday, November 24th
A beautiful day after the rain: the boxes that had been promised did not arrive till late in the afternoon and then were far too big. The largest one we did not want at all and I refused to pay for the largest one, whereupon the Jew who had made them called in the police, who not only upheld my contention, but told me to give him less than I had offered, as I was going to give him too much; excessive greed does not pay. In the morning I went to the Bank of Volga Kama to get some money on my letter of credit: this took

me exactly two hours. Business methods here are not rapid. In the evening Von Brandt, the engineer, came up to see me and produced a most interesting collection of maps and statistics of the district, with all the new irrigation projects, geological maps showing the enormous mineral wealth of the country and others showing rainfall and temperature charts. Besides this he had a very interesting book on the methods of cotton growing in these parts brought out by a large congress on cotton that was held here last year. The rainfall in Bokhara and Khiva is only about 26 per cent and all falls during the winter months, May, June, July, August and September being practically rainless and during July and August, the maximum temperature rises to 42°C. This is the reason why so much irrigation is needed: in the mountains all the summer there is plenty of rain, but none on the plains. Their works consist both of reservoirs and canals and in many places the canals of an earlier civilisation only require digging out. I was astonished at the vast amount of mineral wealth in the mountains between here and China. In Russia there is not sufficient capital to work this and foreign money is badly needed, if the country is to be properly developed. First of all, however, proper roads or railways are most necessary. In the evening we went to the Cinematograph, which again was crowded: the Grand Duke was there and the Governor of Semiretchinsk. I was introduced to Yudin who is the best painter of Turkestan: he has a most interesting face.

Tuesday, November 25th
Another lovely day. I spent the morning in getting the boxes finished and finally I escorted them to the Russian Transport Coy., where I left them and I trust they will arrive safely home. I then went on to the fruit market where I bought some sweet pipless grapes and some peas. It is a large market with many fruit stalls and some very good looking vegetable stalls. There were also a number of birds for sale, chiefly goldfinches: I asked the price of a lark and was told 18 roubles which is five times the amount I paid in Kuldja.

In the afternoon I went with Von Brandt to see Yudin and I bought one or two small paintings from him that were very characteristic of these parts: they were the cheapest paintings that I have ever come across. Just before I was leaving the Hotel, an Englishman, a Mr. Sutherland, asked to see me: I had only a few minutes to spare, so we had a hurried conversation and I found that he had come out to prospect for coal and petroleum. He is the first Englishman that I have seen since leaving Omsk. Our train was late in starting for Samarkand so I had dinner at the station and by tipping the guard I got a coupé to myself.

Wednesday, November 26th

We crossed the Syr-daria in the night and when I woke up we had climbed up to nearly 3,000 feet and were crossing a wide plain at the foot of a fine range of snowy mountains that rose up to the south. We soon descended with extraordinary contrast into the broad and fertile plains watered by the Lerafshan. Rice fields and jheels that looked like good snipe ground, cotton fields and vineyards were on all sides: every inch of the ground seemed cultivated. Just after crossing the Lerafshan we passed a very curious high arched brick bridge. We soon arrived at the station of Samarkand, which is some way from the town.

On arrival I was not stopped by the police, strange to say, though at Tashkent just before I got into the train, I was made to show my passport and say where I was going. I drove to the Grand Hotel, which is kept by a Jew: it seems clean and has a garden where I can put the bear. The climate here is much drier and warmer than Tashkent, though we are a thousand feet higher: the streets are still very dusty as they have had no rain.

I had been given the address of a Sart, who would give me any information I might want: he told me the best shops and we drove off into the old town. Never have I seen such a gaily coloured crowd; everyone here wears coloured puggarees, red, white, yellow, pink and spotted and with long brightly coloured coats, often of regular English wallpaper patterns, with roses or peonies on them, or else they were the curious coloured silks that are made in these parts and which are very pretty. The tout ensemble has an extraordinary richness of effect. The men are tall and good-looking and the glimpses of ancient towers, wooden bazaars and a blaze of colour were delightfully picturesque. The bazaars are inside and all round the great madrassah [mosque school] which with its fine outline of minarets and graceful arches, covered with patterns of the different shades of blue tiles, was quite charming.

The buildings are, alas, not perfect now, though decay has been arrested, but in times of old when the minarets and the domes and all the walls were covered with the most intricate pattern of blue tiles, the effect must have been wonderful. Tomorrow I shall devote the day to examining these old buildings, Tamerlane's tomb and the Bibi Khanum. I bought a few susannies* which are far cheaper here than in India: this seems to be their home, for there are hundreds of them and of the most beautiful patterns, I also bought a few pieces of brass and inlaid work and some very interesting pieces of Persian pottery that are extremely old and which were dug up near Meshed. One bottle is, I think, a very good specimen and the patterns on the tiles are very fine. I was shown also some old Persian carpets and there is so much in the shops in the bazaar that I should like to buy. They are the most interesting shops that I have come across in the East, with the exception of Schwargers at Delhi.

Thursday, November 27th

Soon after nine o'clock we started off on a round of sight seeing: we took a guide with us this time and went first to see Tamerlane's tomb. The tomb of this great warrior is alas but a wreck, and only here and there are a few of the tiles left that recall its former beauty. At the entrance and again round the dome on the tomb itself are a few of those lovely blue tiles that once covered the whole of the buildings, the great arches at the sides are now ruins, but enough remains to show its pristine beauty.

Further decay has been arrested, in the cheapest possible manner, and no attempt at restoration has been made. Within, under the big dome is the tomb of Tamerlane in black marble, covered with inscriptions in Persian and around are the tombs of some of his

---

* Susannies (from *sūzan*, the Persian word for a needle) were linen quilts or wall hangings, some as large as six foot by four, and spectacularly embroidered in coloured silks.

ministers. In the vault below, he and his ministers lie buried. We then drove on to the Registan to the great madrassahs: here again, only a relic of their former beauty remains. Sufficient of the coloured tiles and inscriptions exist to show what a blaze of colour these beautiful and graceful buildings must have been in the days of old. Here I lingered for some time to enjoy and drink in the beauty of the surroundings, the brightly coloured buildings and the equally gaily coloured crowd.

Some of the minarets will I fear not last much longer, as they are already leaning at a dangerous angle; we climbed up on to the roof of the mosque and then on to the summit of one of the minarets by a very steep and dark and narrow staircase. In the old days criminals used to be taken up on to the tops of these minarets and hurled to death on to the ground far below. It must have been a difficult job to get them to the top. A few mullahs live nowadays in these madrassahs and decay has been arrested, though all repairs are cheaply and most inartistically done. The buildings are all of brick, though faced with coloured tiles, and it is a great pity that more stone was not used: in places there are wooden beams running through the buildings.

We then drove on to the Bibi Khanum through the crowded and busy bazaars: though the town is small, there is a great deal of trade done and the people are very rich. The Bibi Khanum, I consider, in the days of its glory must have equalled the Taj in beauty: the immense and graceful arches, the lofty dome covered with tiles that rival the blue of the heavens, the walls still in places covered with inscriptions as fresh as the day on which they were made, the magnificent proportions of the buildings presented a spectacle at which I could only gaze with reverence.

In a few more years but little of these glorious buildings will be left: one great arch over 100 feet in height has fallen, another one has immense cracks along the crown of it, great strips of coloured tiles have separated themselves from the main building and only await a storm to bring them down, in the great dome itself great pieces fall down every year and it is slowly toppling to its ruin. What barbarians the Russians are to leave these buildings thus and to take no steps to prevent their becoming a pile of ruins: late though it is, even now something might be done to prevent their absolute destruction. Outside the walls that enclose these stately buildings was the busy crowd buying and selling and within were the deserted places, shady trees and these wonderful remains of a past grandeur.

The glimpses through the trees of the superb arch and the blue dome beyond was a sight that I shall never forget. It is one of those few visions of perfect beauty that are to be seen during a lifetime. From here I wandered back to the bazaars and then to the house of a rich Persian Jew who gave me tea and fruits and wine. He showed me many things that were interesting, old Persian illustrated books, embroideries that were hundreds of years old and many ancient weapons that delighted me. I only, however, bought a few modern susannies as presents and a couple of fine turquoise belts. The wine that I was given to drink was home made and I think must have had chillies in it as it was hot and very strong: the grapes and apples were, however, excellent and so are the melons of this place: it was not till late that I got back to the Hotel.

Friday, November 28th
There were several more places of interest that we visited in the country around, but their beauty chiefly consists of old buildings with fine shady chenar and poplar trees, and cool ponds: now the season is too late for us to see them at their best. We drove some miles out to an old madrassah, the road was very bad but the fertility of the country was astonishing: everywhere too are fine big trees: how the Russians can want to come to India when they have a wonderfully fertile and rich country such as Turkestan, with an excellent climate and which is only waiting to be developed, I cannot understand. Here are none of the drawbacks that we have in India.

We then drove on to Tamerlane's house of which but little is left now and from there once more to the Bibi Khanum, where I again gazed in wonder and awe at the mighty ruins. From there we went on to the tomb of Shah Zindah. Along the path to it, were the tombs of various relations of Tamerlane's, all covered with tiles of rich design and workmanship: at the end was the tomb of Mahomet's cousin: as there were many people at prayer there I did not stay long but I saw some fine ibex heads and an immense sheep horn on the tomb.

From this place we went on through the old Greek city of Aphrotiab to the tomb of a man who must have been sixty feet long by the length of the grave. In the old Greek city, there is a fine field for the excavator and many treasures ought to be brought to light there. Then back again to the city where I drank tea with a Persian and later on went to the house of a Russian painter and bought a few small paintings of the place.

In the madrassah today it was a fine sight to see the whole pavement covered with people at prayer and their many coloured robes lent and added charm to the already beautiful surroundings. In the evening I went to the Cinematograph, but was not amused: there was a very violent anti-Semite play being shown which was undoubtedly meant to stir up hatred against the Jews.

Saturday, November 29th

I awoke to find a wet morning; my luggage is rapidly increasing in size from the number of purchases I have made. We drove to the station and left by the 10 a.m. for Kagan which is the station for Novi Bokhara and the junction for Old Bokhara. When we got about half way we left the clouds behind us and emerged into brilliant sunshine. The country was flat and wherever there was water, it was extraordinarily fertile; anything grows here: it only needs water.

We passed through patches of apparent desert, but it was only because the ground was not irrigated. Cotton seems one of the chief crops throughout the valley of the Lerafshan and both here and at Samarkand the bazaars are full of it. We got to Kagan about five o'clock and I drove to the Moskovski Hotel. They were very full and I could only get a very small little room. Here I met Major Sykes, our Consul General at Meshed, who had just visited Bokhara and was leaving the next day for Samarkand. As he was going to call on the Political Agent, I went too. M. Giers was away but M. Bloehm was in charge and he and his wife proved most charming and hospitable. He gave me leave to go to Old Bokhara and telephoned for a guide to meet me the next day. We were both invited to dinner and I had the best dinner I have eaten in Russia. Dr. and Mme. Lapitinsky were there too. He had been doctor to the Russians in Seristan and he told me his version of the attempt to enforce quarantine regulations against Indians from India. After dinner we went on to the Club where there was a band and dancing and also badminton and ping pong and it was not till very late that I got back to the Hotel.

Sunday, November 30th
It was a sharp frosty morning: we got down to the station by eight o'clock in order to catch the train to Old Bokhara. This line belongs to the Emir and all the profits go into his pocket. It is only 12 versts long, for which 40 kopecks is charged, so that he makes a very good thing out of it. In half an hour's time we arrived at the station of Old Bokhara: here Usman Khoja Jeveschy, the Chief of the Police in Bokhara, met us in a smart carriage with silvered wheels. He took us round to all the places of interest in the town.

In many ways the place reminded me of a native Indian state, the same outward show and trappings, the same tawdriness and below the surface, and often contrasting with the outward richness, the same poverty, the elaborate silver harness tied up with string, the homely mud beneath the richest of embroideries or language. The city which is of considerable size is surrounded by crenellated mud walls and in the centre of it and rising well above it is the fort in which is the Emir's palace.

The streets are very narrow and tortuous, so that in most places it is impossible for two carts to pass. There are luckily so many side streets that it is usually possible to get round: the houses are all of mud with high walls so that when driving along the streets the vision is very limited. We drove to several of the madrassahs, but they are all very much alike: but few of the tiles are left, though occasional glimpses show that the work must have been very elaborate. In each of the madrassahs was a mullah giving lessons to a large number of grown up pupils. The big Minai from which the criminals used to be thrown, is a fine object and very prominent: from here we went on to the fort, passing on the way the troops returning from parade. There were only a few hundred of them and their appearance was not soldierly or smart: in the rear near the band rode the General, the Commander-in-Chief in a smart uniform with an expansive breast covered with medals and stars.

In the fort there was not much of interest, some good looking but very fat overfed horses, but the buildings for a palace were really pitiable. From here we went on to the Lindan or prison, which is really a raised mound of mud near the fort and in the interior of this are three or four large rooms. There were fifteen to twenty prisoners in each and, on my asking for what reason they were there, was told that anyone that stole, was put there and remained there for the rest of his life. It was only in very exceptional cases when influential friends could intercede for the prisoner that the Emir let anyone out. This method saves trouble to the police and in consequence, with such an awful penalty in front of them, thieves are few. They have all their worldly belongings with them and many that I saw there were playing cards: others came to the iron gates and begged for money.

It was in a dungeon underneath this prison that the two English envoys were thrown many years ago, but this dungeon has now been blocked up. The most interesting feature of Bokhara, however, is the bazaars: these are narrow and tortuous, always thronged by a most gaily coloured crowd: some of the streets have roofs of wood, others of brick and often they lead into an open space covered by a large circular dome of brick, from which four or five streets will radiate. Here a great deal of trade is done and often it is impassable for a carriage: a laden camel is quite sufficient to block the road. The trades are all separate, each has its own bazaar, the carpet sellers, the merchants of silk or khilats, the vendors of hats or susannies, the sellers of cloth, the workers in brass and numberless other crafts, each has its own separate quarter. Scattered also through the town are some most picturesque tanks with stone steps down to the water and overhung by shady trees: round one of these big tanks were barbers' shops all the way round. It would need a life time to learn one's way about the streets in Bokhara, so winding and so similar in appearance are they all.

I then was taken to the house of one Oumidoff who has made a collection of Bokharan curios, and I bought one or two small things from him. I then went back to the station expecting to find a train, but as there was not one for two hours, I walked the 12 versts back to Novi Bokhara and had some lunch at 5 p.m. I then went again to see the Political Agent and drank tea with him and his wife. He was just going off to meet the Emir.

Monday, December 1st
It was a beautifully warm morning and I drove into Bokhara. The country is very like the plains of India: there is the same brown and dusty look about everything. There is however, plenty of water or irrigation and a great deal of cotton is grown. We kept passing strings of camels laden with cotton all the way. Outside the town of Bokhara are the graveyards of centuries and where the ground is covered with tombs there will be two or three layers built one above the other. I spent the morning wandering about the bazaars, poking my nose into all the old and picturesque corners: the long coats that everyone wears here are of the most gorgeous colours, making the scene one of the most brilliant, even in the subdued lights of the bazaars. Many of the bazaars are narrow little passages for foot passengers only, forming a regular rabbit warren in every direction.

In the afternoon we drove back again to the hotel and after packing up, caught the five o'clock train for Merv. This is again the hungry train: there are two trains each way every day: their speed is very much the same, in thirty-six hours one manages to gain an hour, but the great difference is that one has a restaurant car and the other has not. The times of the hungry train have so far been always more convenient and so I have always gone by it: I have to hurry out and buy something at the different stops.

After dark we crossed the Amu-daria by a very fine iron bridge, considerably over a mile in length. The river was quite half a mile in width and seems to have a great deal of water in it. From Charjiri river steamers ply on it both up and down stream. We arrived at Merv at half past three in the morning, but the Hotel was luckily only a hundred yards from the station, so I was able soon to get to bed.

Tuesday, December 2nd

Sleep however, was not for long, as I was up by eight and after breakfast and much bargaining, we engaged a carriage to take us to Bairam Ali which is some 25 versts away. The day was a cloudy one and looked very much like rain, but a strong wind arose from the north, which blew all day with great violence and eventually blew the clouds away. This wind made the drive to Bairam Ali very cold. On the way we passed strings of camels laden with cotton, every few hundred yards led by a Turcoman riding on a donkey and wearing a huge sheepskin hat, which at a little distance looks exactly like the busbies of the guards. The leading camel is always given an elegant headdress in many colours.

The people around here are all Turcomans and wear these curious tall sheepskin hats in either black or brown or white. By character the Turcoman is a delightful person being honest and truthful and their principles are very high. They live in auls, with felt roofs, but the sides are made of reeds. Their women are very proficient in weaving carpets.

The country everywhere was intersected by deep little irrigation canals and a very complete system of irrigation has been arranged: the chief crop seems to be cotton. The road was as usual unmetalled and full of holes and bumps but our horses were good ones and we soon arrived at Bairam Ali. Here we were told that we would have to get leave from the police to see the ruins, so we drove to the office of the chief of the police and he most kindly gave us a government carriage and three good horses.

We first drove through the old ruins of the soldiers' quarters and then through one ruined city after another. But very little was left in most cases except the walls, as everything was of mud and brick, but the ground was one mass of bricks and pottery. Each of these ruined cities must have contained a very large population as they cover an extremely large area of ground. In one of the largest of the cities was the ruin of a very fine tomb of a Sultan: the brickwork in this tomb was exceptionally fine and there was a very fine and lofty dome of brick, which I was very glad to see that the Russian government are repairing.

To the east was a still older city, which must have had walls of immense thickness, as now they form a range of low hills more than a mile square. This city must be about 4,000 years old and to the north-east of it rises what must have been the old citadel. Time only permitted a very hurried visit to these places and then we had to hasten back in order to try and get most of the long drive over before we were overtaken by darkness as the road was very bad. As it was we had to do the last five or six miles in the dark.

Wednesday, December 3rd

I spent the morning in vain trying to buy a carpet: I went to a Persian shop and I saw many carpets, but the train left at mid-day and there was too great a difference between my prices and theirs and we came to no agreement: it would have needed at least two or three days' bargaining. At the station at Merv I was lucky enough to meet Von Brandt again on his way back to Tiflis so we travelled together.

The country was dull and uninteresting: the soil was loess with sand at times, but as the rainfall is very small, scarcely anything grows, though with irrigation any crops might be grown. Towards the south in the evening appeared mountains covered with snow which are near the Persian frontier. It is all Turcoman country through which we are passing and everywhere the people wear huge sheepskin hats and look most picturesque.

Thursday, December 4th

I awoke to the sound of falling rain and on looking out there were grey skies everywhere and what was worse it was blowing a gale. The country was very ugly, bare rocky hills on either side without a tree anywhere. Soon, however, we came to the Caspian Sea, along the borders of which we travelled for some hours: numbers of wild duck were in the sea close to the shore and as we approached Krasnovodsk there were rows of sportsmen lying hidden in the sand waiting for the duck to drift within shot.

Krasnovodsk in many ways reminded me of Aden, the same barren country and rocky hills, the vivid green of the sea contrasting with the bright colours of the hills. It was blowing a gale when we embarked on the S. S. *Kuropatkin*, a very small steamer, in which to make the passage across the Caspian Sea. In the first class there were but few passengers, but the second and third were crowded. The crossing ought to take about fifteen hours, but it took us a couple of hours longer. In the bay of Krasnovodsk it was calm, but once outside the islands, we started pitching terribly and I retired to bed without any dinner.

Friday, December 5th

I did not sleep much during the night as the noises of the deck passengers being ill were disagreeable: I managed, however, to survive myself and towards morning the sea became calmer. It was just getting light as we approached Baku, but the approach was not pretty. It was curious to see the countless oil derricks with steam and smoke belching forth in every direction, but they were not beautiful.

Soon after landing a fire broke out in some houses close to the harbour and all the fire engines in the place rushed up: the outbreak was luckily only a small one and was soon subdued. Having missed the morning train, we had to wait till the afternoon, so to spend the time Von Brandt and I went out to the oil city. Here we found a very obliging manager of one of the oil mines who showed us the whole process, from boring the shaft to pumping up the oil and then separating the oil from the water. It was extremely interesting to see the whole process, but the place seemed a city of mud and oil and the smell of petroleum could never be forgotten a moment. The depth of the oil strata is 250 sagen (1,750 feet) and it takes about three minutes for the plug to come up from the bottom and go down again. On returning to the station, we were in good time to catch the train for Batoum.

Saturday, December 6th

After travelling all night we reached Tiflis in the morning: the country is in parts well wooded and there are some good stag to be found near here. The country is well watered and much water is drawn from the Koura for irrigation. There are two big German colonies from Wurtemburg, who were originally brought to grow grapes for making wines, and they have so prospered that several of the former peasants are now millionaires. The soil is apparently very well suited for the growing of grapes.

Tiflis itself is a fine town and I very nearly stopped there for the day, but with all my luggage I thought it best to go direct to Batoum. After leaving Tiflis we gradually climbed up to about 3,000 feet through broad and fertile valleys, past several most picturesque looking old towns. At times the views of the great snowy mountains were very fine. After passing through a tunnel, we started to descend and entered into another and a damper climate. Here were plenty of rhododendrons in the woods and the vegetation was everywhere much richer. We eventually reached Batoum at one in the morning, over two hours late.

Sunday, December 7th
A beautiful morning and my windows in the Hotel Oriental look out over the bay and harbour of Batoum, across the wooded hills to Elbruz and the distant snows of the Caucasus. It is very warm and mild here and the climate reminds me of a warm Riviera: the vegetation too is everywhere very rich. Tea and tobacco grows here, also bananas and there is a regular semi-tropical vegetation. I spent most of the day in trying to find a steamer that would take me to Constantinople and my bear to England and after much protest and argument I at last found one, a tramp laden with manganese for Garston that would take the bear.

Monday, December 8th
Got my passports visaed and boxes packed up ready to start on the morrow. There are some very pretty gardens here along the edge of the sea which is as blue as the Mediterranean and the views across to Poti with the great snowy chain of the Caucasus behind are very fine. One could certainly have some delightful villas along this coast. The day was a beautifully warm one with a cloudless sky, but I am told that this place has a great reputation for rain.

Tuesday, December 9th
Embarked on the S. S. *Regent* at mid-day and we started off a few hours later in beautiful weather. I have got a very comfortable and

large cabin: the ship is, however, terribly dirty and the manganese dust is everywhere: the food though plain is good. Captain Ramshaw and the officers very pleasant and hospitable. The bear has already made friends with everyone. The ship is a terribly slow one and we only go about 7½ knots. Very fine views of snowy mountains.

Wednesday, December 10th
Rather a swell and an unpleasant motion. Was not hungry for breakfast. Swell however goes down towards evening and appetite returned. Out of sight of land all day.

Thursday, December 11th
Passed Sinope early in the morning and kept near the coast which is rocky with snowy mountains inland. A dead calm all day.

Friday, December 12th
A stormy sunrise but the morning was without wind. At lunch we heard a sea break over the deck and within an hour it was blowing a gale and the fore and aft deck were buried under three feet of water. Seas came right over the bridge. Just before the storm started the bear climbed up to the top deck and refused to come down: instinct must have sent him up, for soon after the place where he had been was swept by seas.

I never saw any ship take so much water. The weather became thick and it was impossible to see the lighthouse at the entrance to the Bosphorus, but we luckily found the lightship and spent the night buffeted by the seas within sight of it. One of the steam pipes of the boiler was broken.

Saturday, December 13th
After an awful night of rolling and pitching, we found the entrance to the Bosphorus in the morning: it was still blowing a full gale and the seas were running very high. The Bosphorus was full of steamers that were afraid to proceed out into the storm, including mail boats. We passed rapidly down the Bosphorus with current and wind behind us, and anchored close to Yildiz Kiosk.

Howard-Bury's expedition diary ends at this point. He has left, however, a ten-page summary of the whole journey, possibly written as a guide to the sequence of the book he was planning to produce. The following is its final paragraph.

The remainder of the journey was plain sailing to Samarkand for a few days, then to Bokhara, then on to Krasnovodsk – across the Caspian Sea to Baku. By train over the Caucasus to Batoum and on by tramp steamer to Constantinople, where the train-de-luxe brought one in comfort to Paris and once more to Western Civilisation and its luxuries. To me at any rate, I think also to most people, whether we walk, or whether we ride or whether we drive, the most abiding joy of travel will always lie in the retrospect. The memories of some days, of some scenes where the world appears altogether too beautiful for us, where we can only gaze in awe and rapture at some marvellous creation of the Almighty, such memories as these are truly a possession which we can treasure as our own and which will remain always to us as a source of inexhaustible pleasure and delight when we look back upon the days of our travelling.

Appendix

*The following notes have survived, compiled by Howard-Bury
in handwriting on Quarter Master General's Division memo
paper.*

TURKESTAN

Notes useful for a journey to Europe via Chinese Turkestan and
Siberia.

Proposed route Srinagar – Gilgit – Kilkik Pass: then via Taghdumbash Pamirs to Kashgar. From Kashgar to Aksu, then across
Tian Shan to Kulga. From Kulga to Sairan Nor, then north-east
to Chugatchak: cross the Russian frontiers and down the Irtish to
Semipalatinsk, thence by steamer to Omsk and back to Europe by
the Siberian Railway.

Srinagar to Gilgit by a good road – special permit required. Is
this road open all the year round for ponies?

Gilgit to Kilkik Pass via Hunja: very bad road: is this passable
for ponies in April or when is the earliest date that it becomes so?
if not is it passable for coolies and cannot yaks be obtained at the
top of Kilkik on the Taghdumbash Pamir?

In Taghdumbash Pamir *Ovis poli* and ibex are obtainable in the
Kukruruk and Bayik nullahs and at Aktash. Go to Tashkurgan,
then on the west side of Mustaghata to Kashgar.

KIT

It is best to hire or buy pack ponies – total number for kit and
riding ought to be between 10 and 15 ponies.

Servants – a good caravan bashi, one syce per 4 ponies, a khitmutgar and bearer combined – one who can speak Hindi and Tursee Persian and Turki – an Argun.

Take one or two 40 lb tents lined with serge – and a couple of smaller tents for servants.

Kit packed in yak dans – presents for Chinese – a few bottles of liqueur and preserved fruit – sweets, etc. – mechanical toys and a few cotton stuffs or puggarees. Total weight of kit ought not to be above 2,300 lb.

MONEY

Russian and English gold are always good: only a little silver is needed.

Indian notes can be changed at Yarhand and Kashgar. A letter of credit on the Russian–Chinese border.

STORES

Slings for rifles and leather covers for gun cases.
Cartridges 200 for each: 2 rifles and 2 shotguns = 800.
Hunting whip.
Good supply shooting boots and gaiters (sambhere): spare nails or screws. Boot trees.
Hunting and skinning knives.
2 Telescopes – 9 snow goggles – 4 or 5 pairs.
Waterbottle and thermos.
Maps.
Warm clothes and coats.
Uniform if possible.
Tents – 40 lb – 2 small ones for servants. Khaki-lined double.
Good bags for packing tents and pointed poles.

Dried fruits and vegetables	Tea
Chocolate	Cocoa
Biscuits	Baking Powder
Worcester Sauce	Keatings
Jam	* Flour

Appendix

Butter

* Sugar

Potatoes *

* Salt – pepper – mustard

Candles and lantern

Porridge

Soup and army rations

Potted meats

Milk

Whiskey and Brandy

Maggi and Beef tea

* Potatoes, flour, sugar and salt can be obtained at most places.

Matches

Cameras and films

Paper, pens, pencils, ink

Toolcases, nails and

Diary book, blotting paper

copper wire and rope

Bromo

Axes and kukris

Cheque book

Money

Table

Waterproof sheets

Chair

Cooking pots

Bed

Plates and spoons

Bath

Mosquito curtains

Hypsometer

Aneroid

Thermometer

Compass

Books to read

MEDICINES

Condy's

Syringe

Thermometer

Plasters, bandages

Cotton wool

Boric powder

Book on Elementary Medicine

Chlorodyne

Castor oil, pills

FOR PRESENTS

Crystallised fruits

Chocolates

Liqueurs

Mechanical toys

Turbans, etc.

Stores to be packed in yak dans.

Index